The Life Journey of a Missionary's Son

ALBERT E. BARNES

ISBN: 978-1-4525-5244-6 (sc)
ISBN: 978-1-4525-5266-8 (e)

Library of Congress Control Number: 2012907150

Balboa Press books may be ordered through booksellers or by contacting:

Balboa Press
A Division of Hay House
1663 Liberty Drive
Bloomington, IN 47403
www.balboapress.com
1-(877) 407-4847

Printed in the United States of America

Balboa Press rev. date: 8/20/2012

BALBOA
PRESS
A DIVISION OF HAY HOUSE

DEDICATION

I proudly dedicate this book to my late dear brother and best friend, Donald Barnes. Working across the political spectrum, Don served as primary Spanish interpreter for seven U.S. Presidents and one U.S. Vice President. His professionalism as an interpreter was top grade, as you see him accompanying all of these presidents on Air Force One flying to several Latin American countries. But Don was much more than an outstanding interpreter. He will always be remembered by his family for all the love he showered on them. I can truthfully say that during his seventy three years on this earth, I never heard one negative word about him.
I will miss you forever, Don!

Acknowledgements

I wish to give thanks to three people that provided invaluable support in writing this book. First and foremost, I would like to thank my life companion, Lovella, for the many contributions she made in helping me write several chapters in my book. I would also like to thank my two stepsons, Juergen, who provided me with my first professional copy of my manuscript, and to Heinz, whose expertise with computers enabled me to prepare and transmit my manuscript to Balboa Press. I am truly grateful for their generous and timely support.

FOREWORD

This is the life journey of an ordinary man who both experienced and witnessed extraordinary events. Between the two covers of this book, you will find an amazing and perhaps unprecedented variety of subjects. You will read the story of a haunted house, dreams that predict the future, the amazing story of my younger brother, Don, who went on to become the personal Spanish interpreter to seven American presidents, traveling with them on Air Force One to Latin American countries. I will present absolute evidence of God's existence. There will be spiritual stories of answered prayers and guidance from Above. You will read about an encounter I had with a Russian Prime Minister. How I was involved in the investigation into the deaths of the three astronauts aboard the Apollo 1 spacecraft at the Kennedy Space Center. I will also describe my involvement in the purchase and use of the first video tape recorder sold in the United States, and how I had control of my own small military air force. Finally, you will read my story of the Universe and the Ant. This book is not only being written for the casual reader, but hopefully, it will offer intriguing possibilities to those who are either atheists or "fence sitters" when it comes to believing in a universe created and guided by Almighty God.

INTRODUCTION

Everybody knows that a woman, following union with a man, creates a human baby in her womb. Human beings, however, have a physical and a spiritual side. A woman cannot create a soul in the womb. Only God can create a spiritual being. The physical side of our self doesn't last very long. Like a suit of clothes, it wears out after 70 or 80 years. Our spiritual side, created in God's image, is eternal, and thus comprises the most important part of our being. If only God can create our spiritual being, is He on standby to create a soul as soon as a man and woman jump into bed?

I will address this question at greater length later in the book, however this question is the greatest mystery of our existence. Knowing the answer would change everything. I have serious doubts that mankind is ready for this revelation. So, should we give it another thought? My answer is yes, because as we contemplate the possibilities, we can dismiss those that lead us to a dead-end. As we think about the subject, we might, like children asking questions, move forward in our enlightenment and understanding. I am not a theologian, (which may be an asset), nor do I present my most intimate thoughts in this book as religious dogma. My idea is to explore these mysteries logically with the intelligence and instincts the Creator gave me. Perhaps I can spark an interest in my fellow human beings to open up their own minds on their life journey.

TABLE OF CONTENTS

CHAPTER 1

THE BEGINNING

My Dad was 9 years old, having been born in Greensboro, N.C., when someone gave him an atlas. Looking at the various continents, his eyes focused on South America. He then took a closer look and saw a country called "Argentina" in the southern part of the continent. With the imagination of a 9-yr old, he made a mental promise that one day he would go to Argentina. Several years later, Dad got a job delivering groceries in a wagon. He was 17, and he soon would meet a 10-yr old girl who would someday become his life companion. The little girl's name was Vera, and the young man's name was Sam. Vera asked Sam if she could ride in the back of his wagon, and he said OK. Several years passed, and then love blossomed between the two. Dad at that time was a member of the "Spring Garden Street Friends Church", a Quaker church in Greensboro, N.C. An opportunity arose for him to attend Malone College, a Friends college in Cleveland, Ohio. Dad wanted Mother to go with him, but Mother resisted the idea. Finally, my Mother gave in, and the two went off. Mother at that time was 17 years old, and was the youngest student at the college. After completing their studies, Dad returned to Greensboro to become the 2nd person to be named pastor at the Spring Garden Street Friends Church. At that time, he received $25 per month from the church. Dad still had the dream of going as a missionary to South America. Unfortunately, the Quaker Church was not sending out missionaries. From a book that had been given to him, Dad read about a church called "The Christian and Missionary Alliance".

This church was founded in 1887 by a very gifted pioneer by the name of Dr. Albert Simpson. (According to Mother, she named me after him). Mother and Dad were married in the Friends Church in Greensboro, N.C. in 1918. Later, they would honeymoon in New York. They both spent 4 months studying at the Christian and Missionary Alliance Bible Institute in Nyack, N.Y. On September 20, 1919, my parents welcomed to this world their first born and named her Sarah Elizabeth. Years later, my oldest sister would adopt legally a nickname: Peggy. At the end of their study in Nyack, Mother and Dad were ready to go to a foreign land and preach the Gospel of Jesus Christ, thus fulfilling one of Jesus' commandments. The church headquarters in New York City wanted to send them to a South American country like Peru or Ecuador where lived a large native population that had never heard the Good News of the Gospel. Dad, however, still had his dream of long ago in his heart, and was finally able to convince the church leaders to send him to Argentina.

Albert E. Barnes

The dream of a 9-year old boy was finally fulfilled. It should be noted that at 20 years of age, Mother was the youngest missionary ever to be sent to the mission field by The Christian and Missionary Alliance. They set sail from New York City on March 17, 1920. Many years of hard work followed, and by January 26, 1930, there were 5 children in the family: My oldest sister, Peggy, (born in the States), followed by my second sister, Ruth, my older brother Sam, then yours truly, and finally my youngest brother, Don. After Peggy, the rest of us were born in Argentina. Mother told me later that the four children born in Argentina were delivered by the same midwife. Her charge was $10.00 per baby, which totaled $40.00 for the four of us. Almost 11 years later, the last member of our family, Ann, would be born in North Carolina. (See family photo). Ann would be the one to follow in Mother and Dad's footsteps, when many years later, she and her husband, Jim, would be sent to Brazil, South America by The Christian and Missionary Alliance Church. The family calling would be continued to a third generation when Ann and Jim's daughter, Debbie, together with her husband Todd, would be sent to Mali, Africa, and then to Indonesia by the same Alliance Church. They are presently still in Indonesia dedicated to doing the Lord's work.

During the 30's, Mother became very active in an organization called "The South American Society of Women". The women's group was founded by a lady named Zona Smith. It should be noted that during these years, the role of women in South American society was a step lower than men's. To this day, women are still considered as "second class citizens" in many parts of the world. This is particularly true in some Muslim societies. In churches, which included The Alliance Church, women had to sit separately from men. When we had guests for dinner, it was considered traditional that at the completion of the meal, all the women seated at the table were expected to get up and withdraw to the kitchen. The men, of course, were left at the table free to discuss "important" matters. It's not difficult to trace this custom back centuries, even to the Bible days. The women in the kitchen were on "standby" should the men at the dining room table need anything, i.e., water, coffee, etc. In this environment, Mother did pioneering work on behalf of women. The Society published a small periodical called "Guia del Hogar" (A Home Guide), and Mother was secretary of this activity. Later on, she became editor of the publication. I'm proud to note that Mother went on to write eight books in her lifetime. She and Dad would ultimately spend 40 years as missionaries in Argentina.

THE BARNES FAMILY (1939)

figure 1.1 i

From left: Ruth, Al, Mother, Dad, Peggy, Sam, Don, Ann

(Note: The picture of Ann was taken several years after the main family photo)

CHAPTER 2

ADOLESCENCE

I was a few weeks old when I made my first trip to the States. Seven months later, on Christmas Eve, we returned to Argentina. During the trip, I developed pneumonia, but Mother said that the salt air cured me.

By the year 1933, I had made 2 trips from Argentina to the States. The trips were made by steamer, and initially took 3 weeks. Having been born in Argentina in 1926, it so happened that it was the year that was scheduled for Mother and Dad to return to the States on furlough. As stated earlier, the second trip was made in 1933 when I was 7 years old. I was at that age where I was looking for excitement. I had explored the ship we were on from stem to stern. When I got to the bow, I was impressed by the strong wind blowing across the deck. I had made friends with a boy my age, when all of a sudden I got a brilliant idea. I got a blanket that people used while lying on a deck chair. I told my little friend to hold one end, while I held on to the other end. This made a great sail. We started on the side where the wind was blowing across the deck. To our great delight, the blanket picked up the wind and we scooted at a good speed across the deck. The only thing between us and the ocean below was a thin rail. We had the sense to drop the blanket before we were blown overboard. The end of this story could easily have been that 2 young children had mysteriously disappeared never to be found. The Good Lord, however, had other plans for our lives. A deck hand saw us, and we were able to make only one skid across the deck. I might add a postscript to this story. I received, what I can describe, as a major spanking from my parents.

When we arrived in the States, Mother and Dad rented a log cabin in a small community called Pinecroft, next to a small lake, not far from Greensboro, N.C. It was there that I experienced a wonderful memory of a story-book Christmas. It was a cold Christmas Eve. Earlier that afternoon, Dad took my brother Sam and I into a nearby woods to cut down an evergreen tree that would become our first Christmas tree in our young lives. There had been a light snow that day. Since Argentina is south of the equator, the seasons down there are reversed from the seasons in the States. Christmas in Argentina was usually one of the hottest days of the year, and we would, more often than not, go to the beach. Because of this, we were left with imagining what a Christmas with snow on the ground would be like. After finding what we thought would become a perfect

Christmas tree, we returned to our warm log cabin. Dad wanted us to believe that Santa Claus played a hand in decorating Christmas trees. We were told that this would happen sometime on Christmas Eve. As it was getting late, and there were no signs of Santa Claus, my older brother Sam and I were sent off to bed. Our bedroom was an attic with two small beds. I remember getting very cold at night as the wind would blow through cracks in the log cabin walls. That night, however, we were so excited thinking about our beautiful tree that we had trouble falling asleep. It must have been sometime before midnight, when we decided to get up and go down the stairs from the attic. As we were on the second floor, we were able to look down on the family room. There we saw a long-to-be remembered sight. My Dad had built a big fire in the fireplace, and was busy decorating the tree. Since missionaries existed on very limited funds, Mother and Dad couldn't afford to buy us presents. What Dad had done was to buy fruit and nuts which he bagged up and hung on the branches of our beautiful tree. Dad never did see us sitting at the top of the stairs. Two little boys transfigured by the scene below. I will always cherish this memory of my first real Christmas.

The next year, 1934, the Alliance Church in New York asked Dad to visit the mission field in Columbia, South America. He still had his heart set on Argentina, but he agreed to make the short trip. Mother in the meantime, was left with 5 small children to plan the return to Argentina. A few months before we left, a strange and tragic event took place. I was 7 years old and my brother Sam was 9. Playing with us was a friend of Sam's, close to his age. They had a B-B gun that had run out of ammunition. The three of us noticed a small wooden shack in an open field near where we lived. We went inside and found a box that had what looked like empty metal cartridges. What we didn't know, was that the abandoned shack once belonged to a road construction company, and the so-called empty cartridges were really dynamite caps used to set off explosives when the road company ran into rock formations. My brother thought that, using a hammer, they could somehow make pellets for their B-B gun. I stuck a handful of the cartridges in my pocket, while Sam and his friend grabbed a few more. We all then went to Sam's friend's house, and, getting a hammer, walked back to the field where earlier we had noticed a big rock. Sam took the hammer and was going to smash the cartridge, when his friend said that it was his hammer and he wanted to do it. Fortunately, my brother and I stood back when his friend swung the hammer down on the cartridge. Immediately, there was a loud explosion, and Sam's friend started to scream. He was holding his hands to his face while blood was running through his fingers. That scared me, and I got up and ran back to our house. I was afraid that Mother would find out about all this, so I emptied my pockets with the shells into a large wooden box in the kitchen that held wood for our kitchen stove. In the meantime, Sam's friend's sister came and when she saw her brother's bloody face, screamed that Sam had shot him in the face. Neighbors called for an ambulance and for the police. The police officer, upon questioning me, found out about the other shells in the kitchen firewood box. If they had been tossed into the stove, the whole house would have blown up, probably killing anybody that was inside. Much later, we found out that Sam's friend had lost his eyesight. That switching of the hammer saved my brother from being blind the rest of his life. Was it fate that played a hand in this tragedy? Shortly thereafter, Mother and the five of us children got on a steamship to Buenos Aires, Argentina. This proved to be the last time we would all be together. All 5 of us kids attended the American Grammar and High School in Buenos Aires. I will only relate a few of the many experiences I had during those 5 years.

Dad owned an old car from the twenties. I believe that it was called a Ford Touring Car. It didn't have glass windows. If you wanted to keep out the elements, you had to snap curtains on fasteners around the windows. For visibility, the curtains had a small center made of plastic that you could see through. Few roads were paved in the province of Buenos Aires, and there were often no bridges to cross the rivers we would encounter during our missionary trips. When we would come to a river that we had to ford across, Dad would ask my sister Peggy, since she was the oldest, to get out and wade across. If the river was shallow enough, he would then drive across. On one occasion, as we approached a river crossing, Dad decided that the water wasn't too deep, making it unnecessary to use Peggy's scouting skills. As we drove across, he realized that he had made a big mistake. The car started to fill with water. He quickly yelled "Abandon ship!" and ordered everybody to get out of the car, and then we watched as our suitcases floated down the river. It took a team of 5 horses from a nearby ranch to pull us out.

Another event took place in 1938. Dad had read in a newspaper that a fleet of large American bombers would be visiting Buenos Aires. He asked me if I wanted to go see them. What a silly question to ask a 12-year old! We then drove to a nearby airport. There lined up on a runway were the largest airplanes I had ever seen. What I didn't know was that the U.S. Army Air Corps had sent six of their newly designed bombers on a good will tour to Argentina. In two days, they covered 12,000 miles. The plane was called the B-17 (See photo). It was built by the Boeing Company in Seattle, Washington. The plane bristled with heavy duty machine guns. When a reporter first saw the B-17, he nicknamed it "The Flying Fortress". I remember telling Dad in awe that nothing could ever shoot it down. Nineteen months later, World War II would start with Nazi Germany invading Poland. Little did we know that the B-17 bomber we were looking at would ultimately help defeat Germany. A total of 640,000 tons of bombs were dropped on Germany by the B-17 bomber. The initial production of 12 B-17's, of which I saw 6 on that day in 1938, grew to a total of 12,731 by the end of World War II.

figure 2.1 [2]

BOEING B-17 FLYING FORTRESS

Another unusual event happened to me when I was 12 years old. We were living in a small town not far from Buenos Aires, where I was attending the American Grammar and High School. That day I was riding a large city bus taking me to where I could walk to the school. These busses had a rear platform where a conductor stood checking the passengers on and off. I remember getting ready to signal the conductor that I wanted to get off. All of a sudden, I was surrounded by a brilliant light. I felt my way to the rear and told the conductor that I wanted to get off. While all this was happening, I was totally blinded by the white light. I remember the bus stopping, my getting out and crossing the sidewalk to the outside wall of a building. I sat with my back to the wall and waited for the light surrounding me to disappear. After a few minutes, I was able to see again. I never told my family about what had happened. I have no explanation for this unusual event, and it never re-occurred.

President Roosevelt's Visit

The year was 1936. Adolph Hitler, the Nazi German dictator, was planning his moves to take over Austria and Czechoslovakia. During most of the 30's, our relationship with South American countries was not too friendly. Latin America experienced many interventions by the USA, who they called "The Colossus From The North". The president of the United States was Franklin D. Roosevelt. Roosevelt thought that a presidential visit from the USA might change the political atmosphere. He planned a trip aboard the heavy cruiser USS Indianapolis. (See photo). His first stop was Brazil, where he addressed the Brazilian Congress in Rio de Janeiro. The Indianapolis then proceeded to Buenos Aires, Argentina. He arrived on November 30, 1936. There he attended a session of the Inter-American Congress. You might wonder how in the world all this would fit in with the life of a 10-year old. Now we get to the most important part of this whole story. The American School that I was attending decided to give our President a rousing welcome. Volunteers were assembled to make large 3 ft. X 3 ft. placards spelling out the words "Welcome President Roosevelt". To this day, I remember holding one of the "O's". Another important part of this event was the presence of the Argentine President, Augustin Pedro Justo. From then on I could claim that I participated in a ceremony that involved two presidents.

figure 2.2 [3]

PRESIDENT FRANKLIN D. ROOSEVELT (1933)

Now for a historical footnote: The USS Indianapolis went on to a very distinguished service in World War II. What no one could foresee was the tragic ending she would experience. The USS Indianapolis, on July 16, 1945, sailed from San Francisco carrying the atomic bomb that was to be dropped on Hiroshima, Japan. Ten days later she arrived at Tinian Island, where she unloaded her lethal cargo. On Tinian was a B-29 Superfortress that was to drop the bomb on an un-suspecting Hiroshima on August 6, 1945. This atomic bomb, nicknamed "Little Boy", would end up killing approximately 100,000 men, women, and children. This number included those who would die later from radiation and injuries.

The following narrative is taken from "The Sinking of the USS Indianapolis, 1945", Eyewitness to History, www.eyewitnesstohistory.com) (2006):

The cruiser Indianapolis, having accomplished her mission to Tinian Island, sailed for the island of Guam. From there she was ordered to go to the Philippines to prepare for the invasion of Japan. Traveling without an escort, her voyage would take her through an oceanic no-man's land infested with Japanese submarines and sharks. Just past midnight, on July 30, two Japanese torpedoes tore into her side, igniting an explosion that broke the ship in two. It took only 12 minutes for the ship to sink, and the US Navy then recorded its worst maritime disaster in US history. Out of an original crew of 1199, only 317 survived. It is one of the great ironies of World War II that the conveyor of the weapon of mass destruction on Japan, would itself be destroyed by a Japanese submarine 7 days before the bomb was dropped on their homeland.

figure 2.3 [4]

THE USS INDIANAPOLIS

While living in Moron (which was near Buenos Aires), one Sunday morning my older brother Sam and I decided that we would go to a small Baptist Church not too far from our house. I was 13-years old and Sam was 15. The minister, through our parents, knew we were missionary's children. During the early part of the service, the church's pastor would invoke the Morning Prayer. Sam and I as always, sat in the back on the left side. We then were shocked to hear the pastor say that he was going to ask Sam to give the opening prayer. As we sat with our heads bowed, not a word was being spoken. All of a sudden, I felt a rustle to my right. I opened my eyes, and to my amazement, saw Sam exiting the church. I sat there petrified. Then in a moment of panic, I got up, and also left the church. As I walked through the door, I could hear the pastor's voice as he started the Morning Prayer. Nothing of this was ever mentioned to my parents. What a relief! My Mother never heard this story until many years later, when she was 88 years old, and Lovella (my fiancé) and I were visiting Greensboro for a Thanksgiving reunion. My Mother exclaimed "My Oh My!", while the rest of the family got a good laugh.

The year was now 1939. The Alliance Church was providing Dad with a new 1939 Chevrolet. A few years before, (1936 I believe), Dad had run across a book written by a man who said that he was the first person to go by automobile from Buenos Aires, Argentina, to the States. The car he drove was a Model "T" Ford. Dad was able to contact this person, during which he described, in great detail, what he had experienced during the journey. The trip over the Andes Mountains from Argentina to Chile was particularly hair-raising. He was able to get up to Columbia, but was then confronted with the fact that roads through Central America were non-existent in many places. This forced him to ship his car by freighter for the rest of the trip. All of these stories fired up Dad's imagination, to the point that he announced to Mother's dismay that he was going to take the family in their brand new Chevrolet on a similar journey. Fortunately, and I do mean fortunately, he found out that Argentina would impose an import fee if he didn't return the car within 12 months. This dissuaded my Dad from making, what could have turned out to be, a traumatic trip for the family of seven. There was one very happy person after all this—Mother.

With the collapse of the automobile idea, Dad started to make plans to return to the states by steamship. On the trip to Buenos Aires in 1936, President Roosevelt noticed that there was a lack of vessels flying the American flag servicing the East coast of South America. When he returned to the States, he decided to rectify the situation and that is when the "Good Neighbor Fleet" came into existence. There would be a total of 3 ships in this fleet, and they would be named, "S.S. Argentina", "S.S. Brazil", and "S.S. Uruguay". We set sail for the States on the "S.S. Argentina" in the spring of 1940. Mother and Dad were on furlough until 1941. At this point, it should be stated that missionaries in the Alliance Church had a 6-year assignment in the mission field before coming home for a one-yr. furlough. Around the middle of 1941, with their furlough coming to an end, they started to make plans to return to the mission field in Argentina. By a strange twist of fate, the ship would turn out to be the "S.S. Argentina". (See photo). The day we sailed out of New York turned out to be a heart-wrenching event. As we moved down the harbor, we passed the Statue of Liberty. Mother and Dad stood at the rails as we passed Lady Liberty. They had a very sad and wistful look on their faces. By contrast, I was overjoyed by the adventure that lay ahead, and couldn't understand why they wouldn't acknowledge my presence. What I didn't realize was that they were saying goodbye to Peggy, Ruth, and Sam, and that they wouldn't be seeing them for 6 long years.

The steamship trips to Argentina took 18 days. To get around the corner of Brazil would actually require sailing half-way across the Atlantic Ocean. Sometime during the early part of the trip, as we cleared the Caribbean Sea, I was on deck when I heard someone yell "submarine behind us!" I looked, and sure enough, there was a submarine on the surface following us about 2 miles back. A great alarm swept through the ship. After all, World War II was in full swing in Europe, and it was common knowledge that German submarines were very active in the Atlantic.

Pearl Harbor, of course hadn't happened yet. Since the United States at the time was neutral, our ship had a huge American flag painted on the sides. At night, large searchlights would bathe the flags in a bright light. As we watched the sub with great apprehension, the captain came on the intercom to tell us that it was a French submarine. We all said a word of thanks for this good news.

On December the 7th the Japanese struck a great blow on Pearl Harbor, disabling all of our battleships. By what some people called a stroke of luck, all of our aircraft carriers were out to sea and escaped the brutal Japanese attack. Our Heavenly Father knew that the carriers would ultimately provide us with victory in the Pacific, and thus were protected from sure destruction in Pearl Harbor. On December 8, 1941 the U.S. Congress declared war on Japan. On December 27, 1941, The S.S. Argentina arrived in New York. All of the American flags on her sides were gone. The ship was dark, as all floodlights were turned off. This would be her last pre-war voyage before becoming a troop-ship in our war against Japan.

figure 2.4 [5]

THE S.S ARGENTINA

Witnessing a Revolution

The year was 1943. For many years, Argentina had suffered through a series of electoral frauds, persecution of political opposition, and government corruption. The decade from 1930 to 1943 became to be known as "The Infamous Decade". Totally oblivious to this chaotic political scene, I was attending the American Grammar and High School in Buenos Aires. It was my senior year, and I was looking forward to my graduation in November. On June 4, 1943, I was in class, when a sudden flurry of activity swept through the school. The teacher in the class I was attending informed us that we had to go home immediately. There was no word of explanation for this abrupt order. When I got home, My Dad, who had been listening to the radio, told us that a revolution had broken out in downtown Buenos Aires. The center of government in Argentina was called "Casa Rosada", which translated means "The Pink House". This building was located in a large plaza in the heart of the city. All we heard was that a very large demonstration was going on in front of the president's house. I was in the kitchen with Dad listening to all the commotion when, to my surprise, he said: "Would you and Don (my younger brother) like to go to the governmental plaza and watch what was going on". We, of course, immediately said that it was a great idea. Mother, on the other hand, was strongly opposed to our going, and thought that it was a bad idea. Well, Dad won out, and off we went. We took a subway to the governmental plaza, and on arrival, saw an ocean of people. All of a sudden we heard explosions in the distance and saw a cloud of white smoke rising into the sky. We found out later that it was tear gas. A short moment afterwards, the crowd in front of us panicked and started rushing toward us. Dad immediately grabbed our hands and pulled us into a doorway, as a sea of people pursued by armed soldiers swept by us. After the crowd passed, Dad took our hands and said: "Well, you kids have witnessed a revolution"! He then told us that this was an experience we would never have the chance of seeing again. After we got home safe and sound, Mother expressed a prayer of thanks that no harm had happened to us. The final part of this story took place behind closed doors between Mother and Dad.

I would like to follow this story with a little bit of what was happening in Argentina at that time. The revolution that I had witnessed was actually a "Coup D'etat", a fancy French phrase for a bloodless revolution. In this case, what happened was that the military moved in quickly and ended the tenure of the then President Castillo. No blood was shed. We heard later that the Naval Academy was possibly going to resist this change, but as far as I knew, this never happened, or it was short lived. From June 1943 to June 1946, Argentina was ruled by a succession of three generals. That is why the 1943 Argentine Revolution was known as "The General's Revolution". All three generals were removed from office by another "Coup". In the background, however, was a colonel by the name of Juan Peron. At the time of the 1943 Argentine Revolution, Peron assumed the position of Secretary of Labor & Social Welfare. Peron became president on June 4, 1946. Peron, and his equally famous wife "Evita" would become world personalities. Both would have a large and lasting influence on the Argentine nation. He ruled for a total of 9 years, then was ousted from office by, again, another coup in 1955. During this period, Evita established her "Eva Peron Foundation". She was politically very active. Through her efforts, women ultimately won the right to vote. With an annual budget of $50 million, she got involved in many construction projects. The most famous of these was the "Children's Republic" theme park which was based on tales from the Brothers Grimm. This was a functioning village that was designed only for children 12 years old and younger. An example of the uniqueness of the design was that doorways were lower than conventional doorways. They were built to allow, only, children 12 years and younger to enter. Street lights were also reduced in size. In June 1951, Evita was to be the vice presidential candidate on Juan Peron's run for re-election. The military, always a dominant factor in Argentine politics, opposed this idea, so she declined the offer. The general public was probably unaware of this, but she was suffering from incurable cancer. Evita passed away in July 1952. A huge period of public mourning almost paralyzed the country. Juan Peron's stature would never be the same, and during his third term as president, he died on July 1, 1974. Evita was 32 years old, and Peron was 78 at the time of their deaths.

figure 2.5 [6]

EVITA PERON

figure 2.6 [7]

JUAN PERON

figure 2.7 [8]

EVITA'S CHILDREN'S VILLAGE

CHAPTER 3

LEAVING THE NEST

The year was 1944. It was a momentous year in the war against Nazi Germany. The Allies, led by General Eisenhower, had successfully landed on what was called "Fortress Europe". Many people thought that this was an impossible mission, but, the right cause won out, and Europe was on the way to being delivered from the Nazi nightmare. At the time, I was an eighteen year old young man, having just graduated from The American Grammar & High School in Buenos Aires, Argentina. I had started work at an American communications company. My real dream was to come back to the States and enroll in our military to serve our country. I didn't dare tell this to my parents, but instead, I told them that I wanted to return to the U.S. to start my college education. This, of course, was one of my aims, but it would have to wait. Since my adolescent years, I had always wanted to be an electrical engineer. As an example of this dream, I will digress from my narrative and turn the clock back to the early 40's. I was around 15 years old. My Dad had long dreamed of opening a Christian & Missionary Alliance Church in downtown Buenos Aires. He located a large house in the city. The house was built in the traditional Spanish style of a two-story structure with the kitchen, living room, 3 bedrooms & a bath located on the ground floor, and 2 bedrooms and a utility room located on the second floor, overlooking a large open-air patio. The roofs in this part of Argentina were flat, since snow was totally unknown. There was a balcony overlooking the patio that connected the rooms. Mother and Dad had a small storage room to the back side of the balcony. During the night time, alley cats would jump across the roofs and try to enter into the storage room. Many nights we would be awakened by the howls of these cats, who were either fighting, making love, or who knows what else. This noisy nuisance was beginning to wear on the patience of my parents. At that time, the budding engineer came up with a brilliant idea. I got a large square wicker basket that had been used to store old clothes. I then took the lid off, and, turning it upside down on the balcony, I propped it up with an old broomstick handle and placed a box of tools on top of it. I then fastened a bare wire dangling down from the center of the basket. On this wire, I fastened a piece of fish from a meal my Mother had just cooked. I then ran a twin wire down to the patio, and into my bedroom through a skylight to a small table by my bed. On the table, I placed a small battery and a door buzzer. I then connected the wires so that anything pulling on the fish wire would complete the circuit to my buzzer. Finally, I tied a cord to the broom handle holding up the basket, and using pulleys, ran it down to my bedside. The great 15-year old hunter was ready for his first prey! I stayed awake for a long time, but nothing happened. I finally fell asleep, when suddenly in the middle of the night, the sound of my buzzer woke me up. I quickly reached for the cord to the basket and gave it a big pull. I heard the clatter of the broomstick hitting the patio floor. This was followed by a loud howl. I then turned over to go to sleep, knowing that my trap had worked sure enough. The next morning, I went up to the balcony. The basket had fallen down, and I heard a loud hissing sound. I had caught my first cat. I then slid the basket into a small room and closed the door. What to do next? I discussed the next step in this drama with my Dad. Even though the cat was smelly and half wild, I couldn't stand the thought of harming him. So my Dad came up with a plan. He gave me a large tow sack and told me to coax the cat into the sack. On Sunday afternoons, Dad liked to take us for a ride out into the countryside. On that particular Sunday we had a small guest on board who was very upset riding in a dark tow sack. We released the cat near a farm house that had a large barn. Believe it or not, during the following days and weeks, I was able to catch 12 cats. I wonder what the farmer thought as he was inundated with 12 angry city cats.

Getting back to my teen story, when I had asked my folks if I could come back to the States to pursue my college education, they were saddened by this request, but both realized that I had reached a stage in life where I wanted to be free to pursue my own dreams. My Dad immediately started making plans for my departure. He first took me to a local police station to get a "Good Conduct" certificate. This was necessary for anyone planning to apply for a passport. Even though my birth certificate was registered in the American Embassy in Buenos Aires noting that my parents were American citizens, and therefore I was American, the Argentine government did not recognize this. I had to get an Argentine passport. In fact, since I was eighteen, I was eligible to be drafted into the Argentine army, even though I was considered by both the U.S. and Argentina to be a citizen of their country. In other words, I had dual citizenship. The important fact, however, was that if I had been drafted into the Argentine army, I would probably have forfeited my U.S. citizenship. This fact added a sense of urgency to my plan to return to the States. After getting my Argentine passport, my Dad made flight reservations for my trip to the good old U.S.A. The night before my departure, Dad held a devotional service for me and the rest of our family. At this time, he opened the Bible to the 121st Psalm. I would like to quote this wonderful Psalm:

"I will lift up my eyes to the mountains; from whence shall my help come? My help comes from the Lord, who made heaven and earth. He will not allow your foot to slip; He who keeps you will not slumber. Behold, He who keeps Israel will neither slumber nor sleep. The Lord is your keeper; the Lord is your shade on your right hand. The sun will not smite you by day, nor the moon by night. The Lord will protect you from all evil; He will keep your soul. The Lord will guard your going out and your coming in from this time forth and forever."

As Dad reached the last sentence, his voice broke. I had never seen my Dad cry before. This was both a sad and emotional moment for all of us. I now was ready to face my big adventure!

The day came for our farewells. It should be noted that I had never undertaken a long trip without Dad and the rest of the family. It was a scary thought, to say the least, as I looked forward to a 6000 mile trip all by myself. Dad had booked me on a flight from Buenos Aires to Washington, D.C. This was to be the first flight ever taken by a family member. The airline was Panagra. This airline was a pioneer in commercial flying. Pan American Airways under the leadership of Juan Trippe had joined with W.R. Grace (a steamship line) to form a new airline called "Pan American Grace Airways" that became to be known as "Panagra". In 1944, the airline flew twin engine DC-3's, a mainstay of the aircraft industry. The trip from Buenos Aires to Washington, D.C. took about 7 days. (They only flew from sunrise to sunset). This was less than half the time it took by steamship. Sixteen years later, a Panagra DC-8 jet would take only 12 hours between the two cities. We took off one day in October and headed for Santiago, Chile. We made a short refueling stop in Cordoba, Argentina. As we came in for a landing, we were hit by a sand storm. The plane was tossed around, to the point that I got airsick. It should be noted, that up to that point, I had made 4 long trips by steamship from New York to Argentina and back, and I was the only family member that had not gotten seasick. Sadly, this great record was about to be broken coming into a landing in Cordoba. After a short stay on the ground, I, or should I say my stomach, regained its composure. As we headed northwest, we could see the great Andes Mountains looming in the distance. Our plane started to gain sufficient altitude to clear the mountain range. To do this we had to climb to approximately 18,000 ft., and the DC-3 was un-pressurized. Before departure, the flight crew had instructed us to breathe oxygen through a tube located by each seat. They recommended doing this if you should start getting dizzy or light-headed. Of course, I was going to prove that I was a man, not a sissy, so I chose not to use the oxygen tube.

We continued to climb toward the mountains. I could see below a snow-covered terrain. It seemed that we were only four or five hundred feet above the mountain tops. By the grace of God, we arrived not long afterwards in Santiago, Chile. We stopped for re-fueling before continuing on to Lima, Peru.

figure 3.1 [9]

DOUGLAS DC-3

We landed late in the day in Lima. After clearing customs, we were bussed to a real nice hotel in downtown Lima. I was told to go to the Panagra office early the next morning, at which time I was given some very bad news. I had lost my seat to priority Americans, who needed to get back to the states as soon as possible. It was my understanding that these passengers were executives from American-owned copper mines in northern Chile. I immediately asked the agent how long I had to wait for a seat on a future flight. He showed me the waiting list of about 50 names, and my name had just been added to the bottom of the list. I was then informed that since I was only 18-years old, and, being that a world war was raging across the planet, my priority status was very low. This wait could take weeks and maybe months. I tried to control my anger and not get into a panic. The money my Dad had given me for the trip was very modest. What to do? Fortunately I knew Spanish fluently. Panagra was not going to pay for my hotel room for more than one day. I had to move out! I then proceeded to scout the neighborhood and was able to locate a small hotel with low rates. I had been advised by Panagra that I only had a 3-day visitor's visa. The first thing I did was to obtain an extension to 30 days. Lima is a beautiful city! I decided to explore the downtown area. While I was walking around the plaza, two good-looking young girls approached me and offered to show me around. I heard a small voice within me (my Guardian Angel?) advising me to decline the girls' invitation. I'll never know how this would have turned out if I had accepted their offer.

I had heard that in Lima, there was one of the world's leading anthropological museums. I decided to go and visit it, since I had plenty of time on my hands. A bus took me to the museum where I was able to examine some of the best artifacts from the Inca Empire. After looking around, I came to a corridor that had a chain across it. I asked a nearby attendant what was behind the chain. He immediately asked me how old I was. After telling him that I was eighteen, he lowered the chain, and told me I could go in to a large room. There were many statues, both large and small. After a closer look, I learned why this room was blocked off. To my great surprise, I found myself looking at what we would now call pornographic people in all sorts of positions. Needless to say, my missionary background is stopping me from any more details. Let me just say that an 18-year old, moderately innocent boy, got a quick education in the sex lives of the Inca people. (Some things never change!)

The next day I went to the Panagra office and inquired whether any seats were available. They said no! I was still on the bottom of the list. It was then that I had a brainstorm. I decided that every hour on the hour, I would go to the reservations counter, and in a very loud voice that the whole room could hear, I repeated these words: "I am the son of a missionary family in Argentina. I was given very limited funds for my trip. I plan to enlist in the U.S. Armed Forces to help my country. I cannot afford to stay in Lima very long. I need you to do something to help me!" I repeated this every hour for 2 days. On the third day, a miracle happened. The reservations agent told me that a vacancy had just occurred, and that I would be leaving tomorrow! I said a silent prayer to the Good Lord and went back to my little hotel. The next day, I found myself flying again, and before the day ended we landed in Panama City, Panama. There, I was told that I would have to share a room with another American man, and that they would only pay for one night stay.

Then I got some really bad news. Because World War II was being fiercely fought in Europe and the Pacific, and being that Panama was an important center for U.S. military being directed to various destinations, I had lost my seat again, and this time it would be for the duration of the war. I couldn't believe what I was hearing. My repeated sad story from Lima, Peru had no effect whatsoever, and I got a very cold shoulder. My spirit was dashed, and I found myself checking into a hotel in downtown Panama City. The only plan I could come up with was to see if I could enlist as a cabin boy on any freighter going to the U.S.. That early evening, my room companion showed up. He was an American business man who had experienced the same thing. Then my roommate, who I later believed was an angel in disguise, told me to get up the next morning at 6 A.M. and then the two of us would take a bus to the airport. He then said that he was going out. I found myself all alone fearing the worst. Then I decided that I too could go out on the town to get away from it all. What I didn't know was that the direction I took was toward Panama City's "red light district". As I walked along, a woman standing in a doorway came out and grabbed me by the arm, saying that she had some "exciting things" to show me. I immediately panicked and broke loose, returning to my hotel as fast as I could. Needless to say, that was the end of my stepping out to see the night life of Panama City.

The next morning, I was ready by 5 A.M. to go back to the airport. When we arrived there, my benefactor told me to go and sit down on a nearby bench, and not to say one word to anybody. He then went to the ticket counter where I could see that he was passing money across to the ticket agent. A short while later, he pointed the agent to me and passed out more money. The next thing I knew, he was signaling me to follow him. We passed through a gate, and there, floating on the water was the most beautiful sight I could ever imagine. It was the legendary Pan American Flying Clipper. I quickly rushed aboard. All the plush seats it had as a commercial airliner were replaced by austere-looking bucket seats. After all, it was war time. At that time, I got separated from my benefactor (Angel?) and never saw him again. Approximately 12 hours later, we landed in the Miami, Florida Harbor.

figure 3.2 [10]

THE PAN AMERICAN FLYING CLIPPER

I went again to the ticket counter and was told that my airline ticket to Washington, D.C. had been forfeited to a G.I. They gave me a train ticket in return. I didn't care one bit. I was just happy that I was on American soil heading to the Nation's capital. I didn't mention at the beginning of this saga that my sister Ruth, and my aunt & uncle, were waiting needlessly at the Washington, D. C. airport, not knowing what had happened to me. Boy, what a story I had to tell them. I grew up in a hurry!

CHAPTER 4

IN DEFENSE OF MY COUNTRY

When I returned to the States in August, 1944, since I was 18-years old, I had to register for the draft. All American citizens of draft age coming back to the States had to register in Selective Service Draft Board No. 1, which was located in Washington, D.C. My aunt & uncle, who lived in Washington, then drove me north to meet with my sister Peggy in New York. While living in Argentina, I had worked for an American company called Standard Electric. The parent company in the U.S. was called Federal Telephone & Radio, and was located in Newark, N.J. Since I planned to work there while I waited to be drafted, my aunt & uncle took me to a small town named Montclair, not far from Newark, where they found a small apartment for me to live in. I felt sure that I wouldn't have to wait long to hear from my Draft Board. In the meantime, I thought that I should fulfill the promise I had made to Mother & Dad in Argentina, that I would return to the States to start my college education. There was a fine engineering college located in Newark. In approaching them for admission, I was taking the first step in fulfilling my long held plan of becoming an electrical engineer. (Remember the story of the wild cats and the trap I devised)? My folks didn't have the resources to pay for my college tuition, which incidentally was fairly modest. After I was accepted at Newark College of Engineering, I got a job on an assembly line at Federal Telephone. I should note that, because of the war, which had been going on for almost 3 years, there was a scarcity of young men. The assembly line was made up of all women, some of them young and good looking. Without going into details, I was asked several times to go home with them for a special dinner. I can state, thanks to my Guardian Angel, that I resisted all temptations. My daily schedule, during this time, was very demanding. I would first get up at 7 A.M., eat a quick breakfast, and then take a streetcar to Newark College. My classes started at 8 A.M., and my last class ended at 3 P.M., at which time I would go to the library and do my homework until 5 P.M. I would then leave the school and head for a nearby diner. After a quick bite to eat, I would catch a streetcar to Federal Telephone and start to work on the night shift starting at 6 P.M. I put in 6 hours on the assembly line, and then at midnight I would get on a streetcar and return to my room in Montclair. This schedule was repeated 5 days/week. I would also put in work hours on the weekend.

The days went by with no word from my Draft Board in Washington. During this time, people around me wondered why I wasn't in uniform. They all thought that I was classified 4F. For a variety of reasons, men in this classification would never be called up. I was placed in this very undesirable situation, having to constantly tell people that I was classified 1A, and was just waiting to be called up. I finally decided that I would go to New York, and try to enlist in the Armed Forces. My first attempt was to try and get into the U.S. Air Force. I located their recruiting station, where I was met with a big surprise. When I submitted my application, I was told that I was too old. For an 18-year old, this was unbelievable! It turns out that the Air Force could only accept 17-yr olds. If you were 18, you were of draft age and had to wait for a letter from your draft board. Because of the major battles being fought both in Europe and the Pacific, the Army was given priority in recruiting draftees. This meant that both the Air Force and the Navy had to wait for a more favorable change in priorities. My disappointment at this news led me to try again. This time I went to a Navy recruiting station. (This decision would ultimately decide what university I would graduate from years later.) The Navy recruiters confronted me with the same news I had heard at the Air Force station, I was too old! As I was walking out I saw a large poster. It said: "The Navy is looking for Aviation Radioman Combat Air Crewmen". I went back in and asked the Navy officer what were the requirements to become a Combat Air Crewman. The position was for the second man behind the pilot in a Navy fighter aircraft. In this position, the combat air crewman was responsible for not only defending the aircraft with a pair of deadly 50-caliber machine guns, but also to communicate with nearby friendly forces. In those days, communication between two combat aircraft relied primarily on radio Morse Code. When enemy fighter aircraft were near, a blinker light would be used, similar to the blinker lights used between two ships. This prevented the enemy from picking up radio signals while using code. Some people cannot master the technique of using Morse Code, so the recruiting officer said that they would give the applicant a short aptitude test. I asked the recruiter if I could take the test, and then wait for a call from the Navy when they could recruit again. He responded that this request was unusual, but seeing that I really wanted to get into the Navy, he would OK it. I found out later, that this two-seater fighter aircraft I would be flying in was named the SB2C Helldiver.

figure 4.1 [11]

THE U. S. NAVY SB2C HELLDIVER

Albert E. Barnes

I took the test, and passed! I was given papers to prove my eligibility. I left clutching the precious papers in my hand. Little did I know at the time that these papers would be involved in a defining change in my life.

I went back to my job and my college studies, and was able to successfully complete my first semester at Newark College of Engineering. It was early spring in 1945, and from the news I was hearing, it became apparent to me that the war in Europe was coming to an end. There was, of course, a full-fledge war going on in the Pacific against Japan. During this time, in the Nevada desert, a destructive military device was being developed which would forever change warfare. The development of this terrible weapon, which would get to be known as the atom bomb, was a deep dark secret.

In the meantime, I was getting desperate to get into uniform. I decided to try and get into the U.S. Merchant Marine. This important element in the war had suffered many casualties at the hands of the German U-Boats in the North Atlantic. I thought that surely they would be in need of volunteers. Since the Merchant Marine was not a branch of the U.S. Armed Forces, I was not limited by my draft age problem. I proceeded to write them a letter requesting admittance into their Midshipman training facility on Long Island, New York. When they found out that I was foreign born in Argentina, they said that I would have to provide proof of my American citizenship. The only proof I had was the fact that my Dad was born in the U.S., and thus I was an American citizen. Dad of course, was still in Argentina. What to do? Well, I decided that I would write a letter to the U.S. State Department in Washington asking for some proof of my American citizenship. On February 14, 1945, I received a letter from R.B. Shipley, Chief of the U.S. Passport Division, attesting to my American citizenship. (See Photo). This letter, incidentally, would serve as my citizenship paper for the rest of my life. I sent a copy of this letter to the Merchant Marine Academy, and waited for an answer. None was forthcoming!

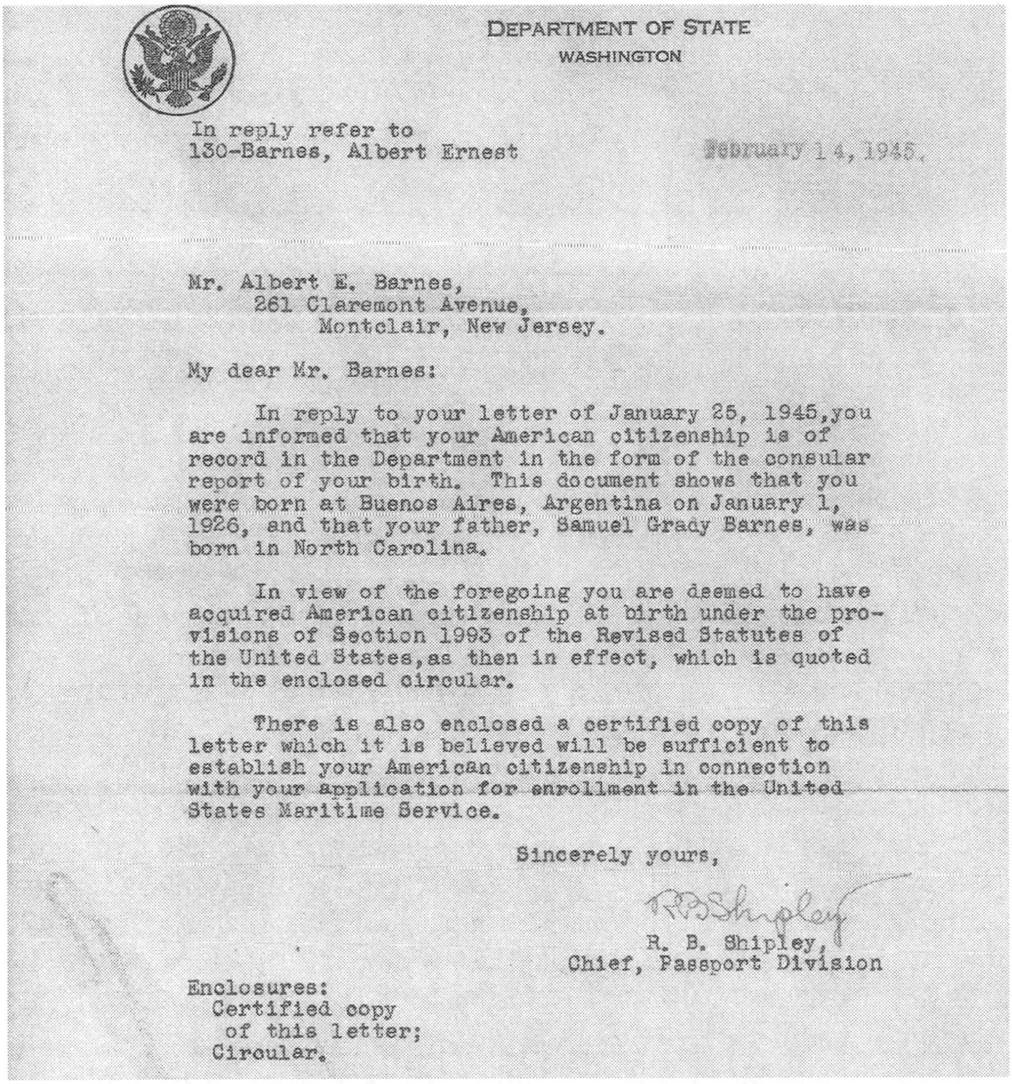

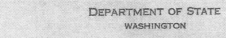

DEPARTMENT OF STATE
WASHINGTON

In reply refer to
130-Barnes, Albert Ernest   February 14, 1945.

Mr. Albert E. Barnes,
        261 Claremont Avenue,
            Montclair, New Jersey.

My dear Mr. Barnes:

        In reply to your letter of January 25, 1945, you
are informed that your American citizenship is of
record in the Department in the form of the consular
report of your birth. This document shows that you
were born at Buenos Aires, Argentina on January 1,
1926, and that your father, Samuel Grady Barnes, was
born in North Carolina.

        In view of the foregoing you are deemed to have
acquired American citizenship at birth under the pro-
visions of Section 1993 of the Revised Statutes of
the United States, as then in effect, which is quoted
in the enclosed circular.

        There is also enclosed a certified copy of this
letter which it is believed will be sufficient to
establish your American citizenship in connection
with your application for enrollment in the United
States Maritime Service.

                            Sincerely yours,

                            R. B. Shipley,
                            Chief, Passport Division

Enclosures:
    Certified copy
     of this letter;
    Circular.

figure 4.2 [12]

MY PROOF OF AMERICAN CITIZENSHIP

Sometime later, after I was inducted into the U.S. Navy, I received a letter from the Merchant Marine to come to Long Island and enter their Academy for midshipman training. Too Late! (Months later, I was to learn that the Good Lord had other plans for me.)

No one in the country, except for President Roosevelt and top administration people, knew about the atom bomb that was being developed. Everybody felt that, ultimately, an invasion of Japan would be required involving over a million men, and probably resulting in a terrible loss of life. The filling of the air crewman positions was badly needed in this war theatre. Still, no word from my draft board: I then did something that I think few, if anyone would do. I wrote a letter to my draft board asking why I wasn't drafted. Three or four days later, I got my long awaited letter, which began "GREETINGS FROM THE PRESIDENT" and then went on to say that I had to immediately report for a pre-induction physical in the Armed Forces Recruiting Station in Newark. I was overjoyed! The next day, I found myself standing in line in my briefs, heading toward an Army

Master Sergeant sitting at a large table. Beside him was a Navy Chief with his legs propped up on the desk reading a newspaper. In my hand I was clutching the Combat Air Crewman papers I had obtained months before. As the line moved forward, I realized, to my alarm, that I was heading straight into the Army. When I was 5th from the sergeant, I jumped out of line and went to the Navy chief. Pulling down his newspaper, I said "Chief, I'm ready to join the Navy!" Immediately, the Army sergeant barked: "Get back in line, recruit!!" The Navy chief then said: "Wait sergeant, you've been taking men for days, let me talk to this one." The sergeant grumbled "OK". The Navy chief then read my papers. Everything was in order. He then got a stamp and stamped "U.S. NAVY" on all my papers. It had been 9 months since I arrived back at the States. I was finally going to be in uniform and fight for my country. The date was May 12, 1945. Four days earlier, the war had ended in Europe.

There was, however, a big war going on in the Pacific. After my induction was completed, I was sent to a Navy training center in Memphis, Tennessee to start my boot-camp training. My starting rank was "Seaman 2nd Class". Boot-camp had a 6-week duration. During this training period, I learned radio code, including blinker light and flag codes. The hardest one to learn was blinker light. This was a handheld light with which you hand-operated a shutter to send out Morse code. This method of communications was extensively used between ships during combat. As a combat aircrewman, I was to use it during preparation for battle. I quickly passed the radio code finals, and then I was told to report to an assembly room to take the blinker light test. I didn't feel confident as I entered the room. I then noticed that the seaman operating the blinker light was sitting at the front of the room. Suddenly, I had a brain-storm. What if I sat near the blinker light? I could hear the clicking of the light, which would help me read the code. It worked, and I finally passed all my required tests. The following week, I was to be transferred to another Navy center for training with a live 50-caliber machine gun before joining an SB2-C Helldiver pilot for final training. After this training period, I would be transferred to the Pacific War Theatre. While I was awaiting my departure from Memphis, I happened to read a notice on the recreation hall bulletin board announcing that the Navy wanted to recruit candidates for pilot training. (Divine guidance was, once again, taking a hand). Becoming a Navy pilot sounded like a great opportunity. About 100 young men took what was equivalent to a college entrance exam. I, together with 25 other applicants, passed the exam. Then something unusual happened that would decide where I would complete my college education. Our supervisor took the list of 26 names and then announced where we would be going for our university studies. The first 6 names would go to Duke University in Durham, N.C. Since my name began with a "B", I found myself in this first group. What a wonderful turn of events, since my family was all from North Carolina. Just for the record, the next 6 named would go to Union College in upstate New York, followed by 6 assigned to Penn State University. I don't remember where the final applicants went. When I arrived at Duke University, I was placed in a pre-flight program known as V-5. Before I could go into pilot training, I was required to complete 3 semesters of college. Since I had completed my first semester at Newark College of Engineering, I needed 2 more. My dream was still to become an electrical engineer, however, this would have to wait until the end of the war in the Pacific. As noted earlier, the nation was unaware of the development of the atomic bomb, and knowing the tenacity of the Japanese, I felt that there was still time for me to help out in the Pacific. Meanwhile, I found out that the V-5 Program at Duke, had a competitor in establishing priorities. This program was called V-12, and was designed to supplement the availability of commissioned officers in the Navy.

Several well-known celebrities attended this program. These included, (and what they would become): Howard Baker (senator); Scott Carpenter (astronaut), Johnny Carson (TV personality); Warren Christopher (Secretary of State); Jackie Cooper (actor); Robert F. Kennedy (U.S. Attorney General); Jack Lemmon (actor); Patrick Moyniham (Senator); Pierre Salinger (Presidential Press Secretary); and many more too numerous to mention. And then there is the V-5 Program and yours truly. Unfortunately, the V-12 Program had priority over my program, so they had first choice on college subjects. This meant that they were signed up for most of the science and math subjects, and I would have to be content with Liberal Arts courses, such as Psychology, English, Religion, etc. Since the V-12 candidates were attending the very classes I was interested in, I would have to make up for this in the future to complete my engineering curriculum. Strange to say, my Liberal Arts subjects would help me in my career, particularly when I entered into management positions, as they aided my skills in both verbal and written communications. One unusual experience that occurred while I was at Duke involved my one-man protest over discrimination of African-Americans (called "Colored" in those days). On a visit to the nearby town of Durham, N.C., I boarded one of the city busses and walked to the rear, where I noticed there were several empty seats. The bus driver immediately told me I had to move to the front of the bus where the white people were sitting. I told him that I was all right where I was. In an angry voice, he said: "We are not moving until you come up to a front seat."

Since I was in a Navy uniform, and not wanting to create a scene, I moved to a front seat. That night, in my dormitory, I found myself getting very angry over what I had experienced. I then decided to write a letter to the editor of the local "Durham News". A few days later, my V-5 officer-in-charge called me to his office. In his hands was a copy of the newspaper. "What is this?" he asked pointing to the "Letters to the Editor" section. I told him about my experience on the bus in Durham. He immediately said: "Sailor, you don't have the right to involve the Navy in a protest of a local law. You are ordered to cease and desist from any more letters to a newspaper editor". I wanted to quote to him the "First Amendment" in our Constitution, but then I thought that I better not. The year was 1945. This was 10 years before Rosa Parks, who was to become a famous civil rights activist, refused to give up her seat to a white passenger in Montgomery, Alabama. There is no comparison in the stories, however, since she went on to start a major freedom of equality movement.

I completed my required V-5 Program college studies at Duke University, with the exception of 2 final courses. For unknown reasons, the Navy sent me to Columbia University in New York City, where I took a course in both inorganic and organic chemistry, thus completing the necessary credit hours for the V-5 Pilot Training Program. I was then transferred to the U.S. Navy reserve training base at the Naval Air Station in Dallas, Texas. On August 15, 1945 fighting in the Pacific war theatre ended with the dropping of two atomic bombs and the surrender of Japan.

The year was now 1946,and my long quest to get into uniform and fight for my country ended. In September of 1946, I applied for a discharge under the U.S. Demobilization Act then in force. My short military career ended on Sept. 9, 1946.

figure 4.3 [13]

PROOF THAT I WAS IN THE U.S. NAVY (1945)

CHAPTER 5

MY COLLEGE YEARS

After completing my first semester of college at Newark College of Engineering, and then 2 semesters at Duke University, and then discharged from the Navy in 1946, I was ready to resume my goal in achieving a degree in Electrical Engineering. I immediately applied to Duke University for admission to continue my engineering studies under the G.I. Bill. This great college financial assistance program, passed by the U.S. Congress, would provide me with the necessary funds to complete my education. I was told by Duke, however, that I would have to wait one semester because enrollment had reached capacity. Once again I was faced with a pause in my pursuit of an engineering degree. My sister Ruth and her husband, Jimmy, lived in Washington, D. C. where Jimmy was pursuing an advanced degree in speech. Ultimately, he would get his PhD and become Dean of the Speech Dept. at Ohio State University in Columbus, Ohio. Before this was accomplished, I stayed at Ruth's apartment. I was able to obtain a job with the Veterans Administration, and started night school at George Washington University. The following year, I returned to Duke University and completed my academic requirements toward my engineering degree. I thus had attended four universities in achieving my scholastic goal. If nothing else, I deserved an "A" for perseverance. I would like to relate a personal "Huckleberry Finn" type of experience in my life that took place before I graduated. The year was 1947. The spring semester at Duke had ended, and I had about 2 months free time on my hands. I decided to apply for summer employment at the Duke Power Co. The person who interviewed me said that he didn't have any temporary positions available. He then told me to check back with him after graduation. Years later, it became evident that working for a power company was never to be in my future.

I then made a decision that would provide me with a great adventure for that summer. I contacted two old friends I had met in the Navy. At that time, I was the proud owner of a 1934 Master DeLuxe Chevrolet. I asked my friends if they would be interested in making a 3200-mile trip to Fairbanks, Alaska. Without a moment hesitation, each said "Sign me up!" There was one tiny problem. We didn't have any money. Between us, we were able to come up with enough money to buy gasoline and food (mostly canned beans, soup & bread). Occasionally, we would splurge and buy a can of corned beef hash. Staying in motels was out of the question, so we bought some inexpensive sleeping bags and a couple of blankets, and off we went, heading west from New York City. The three of us, interestingly, represented 3 major religious groups. I, of course, was Protestant; Bob, the second member of our group, was Catholic; and Rube, the third member was Jewish. Quite a mixed group! We called ourselves "The Fearsome Threesome". We decided that we would drive until we ran low on gas, food and money, and then we would look for temporary jobs. The word "temporary" meant 5 days max. The first day out, we reached a farm in Ohio. This farm had a very large barn, so we asked the farmer for permission to spend the night in his barn. We told him that we were college students on summer break. He readily agreed and he generously invited us for breakfast the next morning. At the crack of dawn, we knocked on his door and were invited in to partake of a large country breakfast. No sooner had we sat down, when 2 young good-looking girls asked if they could join us. We readily agreed and enjoyed chatting with them as we ate. Towards the end of the meal, the farmer asked us if we were interested in a summer job. We looked at the girls, who were neatly dressed in their Sunday best, and realized why we had been invited for the early morning meal. Without hesitation, we thanked him for his hospitality and quickly got back on the road. That was a close call! A few days later, we reached Kansas. To us, the state was one big wheat field. Toward the end of the day, we started looking for a place to spend the night. We decided to pull off on a small side road just far enough not to be seen by anybody on the main road. We then flattened the wheat in a small area, and laid down our sleeping bags. At this time we began to be concerned about our safety at night. What if someone saw our car and decided to either harm us or take our car, or both. We did have some weapons with us. My friend Bob had a .22 caliber rifle, Rube had a more potent 30-30 caliber rifle, and I had a small hatchet. All of a sudden, I remember waking up and, in the moonlight, seeing a bearded face peering down at me. I jumped up and let out a loud yell. My two buddies immediately leaped out of their sleeping bags and grabbed their rifles.

In the meantime, I got my flashlight and my hatchet, ready to repel all boarders. The bearded man then started to run away from us. My two friends quickly got off a couple of shots over his head. Our midnight marauder, meanwhile, had taken off at great speed, and probably did not stop running for a couple of miles. That night, we decided that we were too vulnerable sleeping with our car parked nearby. As a budding electrical engineer, I came up with an alarm system. We went to a small hardware store in the next town and purchased the following items: one cheap old fashioned door bell, a lantern battery, a roll of bare wire, and several small wooden stakes. That evening, before we went to sleep, and using the wire and stakes, I made a large double-wire circle around our sleeping area. The wires were not touching each other. I then connected the bell and battery to the wires so they would ring the bell by anybody brushing against them. After we went to sleep and just before dawn, the bell started ringing. We all jumped up ready to defend ourselves when, we noticed a little black dog had tripped the alarm. (You can see him in one of the accompanying pictures). Everybody, including the dog, had a big laugh!

From Kansas we headed west to Colorado, and crossed the continental divide at "Rabbit Ears Pass". From there, we continued west to Salt Lake City, Utah. In Salt Lake City, we visited the world famous "Mormon Tabernacle". We then went on to "The Great Salt Lake" where we experienced floating in concentrated salt water. By this time, we started to run low on funds. A short distance from Salt Lake City was a small town by the name of Tooele. Near the town, there was a company named "International Smelting & Refining". The three of us applied for work, and we were immediately hired. We soon found out that we could work both a day shift and a night shift. Wanting to make money as quickly as possible, we signed up for the double shift. Later, we would learn what it was like to be a convict sentenced to hard labor. The day shift consisted of taking a 16-pound sledge hammer and walk along the top of iron ore freight cars looking for chunks of ore that would not fit in the crusher. Looking at us stripped to our waste, in the hot sun, breaking up iron ore, and you can see why I equated this with convict hard labor. Somehow, we survived the physical ordeal. Fortunately, the night shift did not require physical exertion. When we reported to the night shift foreman, he gave us a choice of 2 jobs. One job entailed watching the belts that conveyed the crushed iron ore to the smelting ovens.

The only thing we had to do was stop the belts if they jammed up. After clearing the jam, we would restart the motors driving the belts. The only drawback to this job was the constant cloud of dust around us. We were provided with dust masks which helped some. Rube and I volunteered for the belt supervising job. Bob, on the other hand, chose what was called supervising the "biscuit machine". The biscuit machine was comprised of a 4-ft wide steel segmented belt that carried the red hot slag from the smelter and dumped it into open freight cars. Bob thought that this would be the more interesting job. Little did he know what he was getting into. During the first break period, Bob came back to us shaken up and said: "I know what Hell is like". It turned out that the job entailed walking on a wooden board walk overlooking the railroad cars, and signaling when the cars were full of the red-hot slag. To his great surprise, as the slag fell into the open railroad cars, occasionally, a large flame would flare up.. When this happened, the flame would sometimes ignite the wooden catwalk. At that time, he had a fire extinguisher to put out the flame on the catwalk. The smell of sulfur in the air didn't help. Not surprising, Bob never returned to the biscuit machine job. That first night, we took our aching bodies to a cheap rooming house we had found when we first arrived in Tooele.

figure 5.1 [14]

INTERNATIONAL SMELTING & REFINING COMPANY

The next morning, to our surprise, we found a parking ticket on our windshield. It said that we were parked illegally, and were told to report to the traffic judge. We thought a great injustice had been done, since we did not see any "No Parking" signs. The judge said: "Didn't you hear the 8P.M. curfew siren that prohibited parking on the town streets until morning?" When we protested that we didn't know about this regulation, and besides, we had been working a double shift at the smelter, he said: "Boys, its only $10 dollars". We paid the fine. After 5 arduous days of work, the three of us had made enough money to say goodbye to Tooele.

figure 5.2 [15]

MY TRUSTY 1934 CHEVROLET

(My younger brother Don behind the wheel)

figure 5.3 [16]

THE FEARSOME THREESOME

(Bob - Rube - Yours Truly)

figure 5.4 [17]

MOUNT RUSHMORE

figure 5.4a[18]

OUR LITTLE BLACK DOG

figure 5.5 [19]

RUBE & BOB

(Crossing The Rocky Mountains in Colorado)

figure 5.6 [20]

COULD IT BE INDIANA JONES?

(Nope! It's Yours Truly)

figure 5.7 [21]

RUBE & FRIEND

(Dead Rattlesnake)

Our next destination was Glacier National Park in northern Montana. From there, we planned to cross into Canada, and connect with the "ALCAN HIGHWAY" which would ultimately take us to Fairbanks, Alaska. This road, which was gravel at the time, was built during World War II to connect the lower part of the United States to Alaska. It extended for approximately 1400 miles, and was completed in 1942. When we arrived at the Canadian customs check point, we immediately met with a major obstacle. The Canadian officer asked us where we were going. We told him that Fairbanks, Alaska was our destination. He looked at my old Chevy and said that he would need a $300 bond to ensure the return of our car back to the States should it break down along the ALCAN HIGHWAY. He might as well have asked for $3000. At that moment, our dream of going to Alaska ended. (A small footnote: The ALCAN HIGHWAY is now considered part of the PAN AMERICAN HIGHWAY that extends from Fairbanks, Alaska to Buenos Aires, Argentina).

The next part of our journey took us south to California. On the way, we stopped at the Grand Canyon to take in its grandeur. We then continued our trip to California. Not far from Los Angeles, we came to San Bernardino, a city located in a hilly region of California. By the time we got there, once again, we were running low on our financial resources. We found that the city was having a new sewer line installed and had openings for healthy, muscular men. We immediately took the job offer. There was, however, one small requirement. We had to join a labor union called, unbelievably, the "Ditch Diggers Union Of America, CIO". We, of course, signed up, and for the first and only time in my life, I had joined a labor union. Little did I know that this membership and job would last a little under three days. We were told to report for work at 7A.M. the next day. When we arrived at the work site, I was given a wheelbarrow to haul away the soil being excavated. I was the lucky one! My two friends were given shovels and told to start digging. For the next two days, we worked, half-heartedly I should admit, in digging for the new sewer line. On the 3rd day, our foreman came over to us and told us in no uncertain terms that he didn't like our work. One of my friends, and I won't say who, sounded off. It took only seconds for the three of us to be fired. Fortunately, we got paid for three days work, and they refunded our membership fees in the labor union. As we left, I could hear the foreman yell that this would be the last time that he would hire college students.

Once again, we hit the road, and before long, we arrived in Los Angeles. We did some sightseeing and started thinking about where we would be sleeping that night. I remember seeing a highway sign indicating that Long Beach wasn't too far away. Sleeping on the beach sounded like a great idea. We could already hear the soft sound of waves rolling on to the beach. We arrived at Long Beach before dark, and cooked one of our remaining cans of our gourmet food. Later that evening, we opened our sleeping bags and settled in for the night. It must have been around dawn the next morning when I was awakened by a jab in my side. I looked up and saw a uniformed guard. He barked: "We don't allow bums on our beaches!" The three of us got up and yelled back at him that we were college students on a summer break. To make matters worse, we had let our beards grow out, and we definitely did not look like students. We then told him that bums did not travel around in a car. He started laughing until I pointed to our 1934 Chevy parked on a side street not very far away. He didn't believe that it was our car. At that moment, my friend Rube, who was attending New York University and was majoring in Philosophy, started a discourse on the two great German philosophers Goethe and Kant. That did it, and he told us to enjoy the beach. We thought that this was a good time to discuss our future plans. The biggest disappointment of the trip was our inability to drive on to Fairbanks, Alaska. Then I came up with one of my brilliant ideas. Why don't we head for Mexico City! We still had about a month left in our summer break. It didn't take too much convincing, so that the next day, we were on the road again, heading East. One of the threesome wanted to go by way of Oklahoma City, so we headed in that direction.. When we were about ½ day's journey away, it was beginning to get dark. As usual, we were almost stone broke. Our car's insatiable appetite for gasoline had consumed most of our money. We felt certain that Oklahoma would surely provide us with temporary jobs. We were facing, however, an immediate problem. No food! At that time we were driving through a small town, and noticed that a bakery was advertising day-old bread at half price. We went into the store, where we were waited on by a pretty young girl. She told us that the bread normally sold for 60 cents, but she would let us have a loaf for 30 cents, we counted our money and could come up with only 25 cents. We turned to leave, when she suddenly called us back. She had just been informed that the price had dropped to 25 cents. We smiled and gave her a big thanks. As we drove toward Oklahoma City, it started to get dark. We noticed a small woods and decided to spend the night there. One problem! We were hungry. Again, all we had was a can of beans, and our newly purchased loaf of bread. Bob came up with a great idea. We had noticed some squirrels running around through the trees. The idea of eating roast squirrel did not appeal to me too much, but, as the old saying goes, "beggars can't be choosers". Bob got out his trusted rifle and tried to bring down a squirrel. No such luck. Then I noticed a nearby large bird. This time Bob was luckier, and the three of us celebrated his amazing marksmanship. We looked at our dinner lying on the ground, and noticed that Bob had killed a large woodpecker! I won't go into details on how we cooked our dinner, but for the record, those were the smallest and toughest drumsticks I had ever eaten. To this day, I can't look a woodpecker in the eye.

When we arrived in Oklahoma City the next day, we immediately went to the state employment office to see if temporary jobs were available that would pay daily for a day's work. They said that a war surplus store needed night shift help. (I might add that World War II had ended only 2 years before, which meant there was a huge amount of surplus war items ready for retail outlets.) We immediately went to the store and they hired all three of us. The job we were given was to organize a large pile of military aircraft parts, separating hydraulic items such as pumps into one pile, and electrical items into another. When we finished segregating the parts as directed, we were told to organize them in a different way. It became obvious to us that this was a "make work" job. We didn't care, and late that evening we got our first pay. Since it was getting late, we decided we would go to the nearest motel to spend the night. We found a very inexpensive one not far away. It turned out that this motel was "seedy" to say the least. It had a community bathroom on each floor. As we were walking toward our room, a nearby door opened, and a totally buff- naked woman ran out toward the bathroom. I can't say that we turned our heads, and did not take this sight in. Oh well, so much for my missionary upbringing!

The next day, we went back to the state employment office to see if they had any jobs that we could work during the day. It was our plan to work both a day shift and a night shift. The employment office informed us that near the city was a large Air Force base called "Tinker Field". The air base was always looking for unskilled labor. We drove out to Tinker Field and all three of us were hired on the spot. The title we were given was "Crater Carpenter Helpers". Translated, this meant we would be making wooden crates. We continued to work the two jobs for several days. One day on the way to Tinker Field, I glanced at my rear view mirror and noticed something unusual. The car behind us had double wooden front bumpers. I remember reading somewhere that the last cars coming off the assembly lines after Pearl Harbor had wooden bumpers to conserve on steel. I didn't think any more about this until I noticed the same car following us on the way back from Tinker Field. I mentioned this to my two friends that I thought somebody was following us.

They just laughed until I started to try and shake off our mysterious rear companion without much luck. Finally, they turned away as we neared our night-time job location. As we checked into the store, to our surprise, they had us doing some of the same dumb things we had experienced the night before. The next morning, history repeated itself, except that this time, our wooden bumper car suddenly sped up and forced us to the side of the road. As soon as we had stopped, four men in business suits jumped out of their car. One went in front of our car, one in back, one to our right side, and one came up to my window. I didn't know what to think, but I was badly shaken up. As I waited, the man at my window asked me where we worked. I responded "Tinker Field". Then he asked me if we worked anywhere else. We told him about our war surplus parts job. He seemed very interested in our night job, and asked me for the address. I told him, and also described the unusual happenings we encountered in the shop. He was very polite and thanked me for the information. Not once did I ask him who he was. After that, we never saw them again. Later, we talked about our strange encounter, trying to figure out what the incident was all about. We concluded that they couldn't be part of the local law enforcement police, since they didn't ask for our ID. They were probably Federal government agents looking into, for unknown reasons, our night time employer. We will never know the true story.

With the two jobs we had worked in Oklahoma City, the three of us were able to save up a fair amount of money. One expense that we had to make before heading to Mexico was to buy two badly needed new tires. We went to Sears & Roebuck and purchased two of their cheapest tires, and had them installed on our rear wheels. The tires came with a 12-month warranty. Little did we know that a week later we would be using this warranty. Leaving Oklahoma City, we headed south towards Laredo, Texas. There we crossed the border into Mexico, and found out to our surprise, that the road to Mexico City was a first-class paved road. It took us two days to drive the approximately 700 miles from Laredo to Mexico City. While in the city, we visited some of the well-known tourist spots, including the National Palace, the old cathedral in the center of town, the Latin-American Tower, and several other places. We soon became anxious to resume our travels in my trusty 1934 Chevy. For those who don't believe in Guardian Angels, the next story should convince even the hardest skeptic. Before leaving Mexico City, we spoke to a casual acquaintance to see if he recommended any sights south of the city. He immediately said there was a volcano about 50 miles south of Mexico City which was worth seeing. The name was Mount Popocatepetl, which is Aztec for "Smoking Mountain". The locals call the volcano Mount Popo. The mountain is 17,800 ft. high, and this makes it the 2nd highest peak in Mexico. It is also one of three tallest peaks in Mexico to contain glaciers. What our Mexico City friend didn't tell us was that Mount Popo was actually an active volcano. At the time, luckily, it happened to be dormant! Without further ado, we headed south, arriving about an hour later to the base of the mountain. There, on the left from the main highway we were on, was a small paved road leading towards the mountain. As we drove down the road, we started climbing. Without knowing for sure, we must have climbed several thousand feet.

figure 5.8 [22]

MOUNT POPOCATEPETL

The road suddenly ended upon reaching a small guard house. We looked inside, but there was no one home. We then noticed that the road continued up, but it was unpaved. We took a quick vote and unanimously agreed to continue to climb. Little did we realize that this decision could easily have ended up in a major tragedy. The road started getting very narrow, to the point that it was one lane wide. To the right was the wall of the mountain and to the left was a sheer drop down the mountainside. As we climbed, we passed a small indentation in the side of the mountain that was probably used by the road construction crews. It would soon save our lives! There were two major problems ahead. Our wheels started to spin as we began to lose traction because of volcanic ash on the road. To further compound the danger, fog started to form. We immediately stopped our climb. To the left we knew there was a sheer drop down the mountainside. There were, of course, no guard rails. My two friends got out of the car: one on the left front and one on the left rear. Slowly we started to back down, looking for the small indentation in the side of the mountain. Finally, after what seemed an eternity, we spotted the little cut a short distance below where we were. Gingerly, with "flies in my stomach", I backed the car into the work area and was able to turn around. What we didn't know, was that this road was considered unusable for automobiles. This is where our Guardian Angels come in. When our car started to skid, we could easily have gone over the side. There wasn't a soul on earth that knew where we were. Even the drive down to Mexico was unknown to our families. We would have mysteriously disappeared off the face of the earth, never to be heard from again. It is doubtful that even our bodies would ever have been discovered. There is no question that the Good Lord had other plans for our lives! But, that isn't the end of the story. We were heading back to Mexico City, when all of a sudden, one of the new tires that we had purchased in Oklahoma City blew out. Fortunately, again with help from Above, I was able to bring the car to a safe stop. My 1934 Chevy has two spare tires mounted on each side of the front of the car. We quickly changed the flat and we were once again on our way. As we neared Mexico City, I began to think of our 1-year warranty on the two tires we had bought earlier in Oklahoma.

Could it be possible that there was a Sears & Roebuck in Mexico City? Sure enough, one had recently been built near the center of town. We went to the auto service dept. and told of our story with the tire. As the service man looked at our damaged tire, he noticed that something had cut the side. Then he said something that I'll never forget. We received a warning not to go off any unpaved roads near Mt. Popo because there were slivers of glass in the volcanic ash which could damage tires. Fortunately, he didn't ask us if we had been there. All three of us thanked him for his advice, as we drove off with a brand new tire. That ended any desire to further explore Mexico. There were two roads that went from Laredo to Mexico City. One was the road that we first took, that later would become part of the Pan American Highway, which, as mentioned previously, would extend from Fairbanks, Alaska to Buenos Aires, Argentina. I would like to point out an unusual fact. This was the third involvement in my young life with the Pan American Highway. The first was my Dad's desire in the '30's to drive from Argentina to the States; the second was our attempt to drive to Alaska, and the third was our trip to Mexico City. We were now confronted with two choices. Should we return by the Mexican Pan American Highway, or should we go by an eastern route that hugged the coast. Of course, we chose the new route. To our surprise, the inhabitants we encountered were mostly native Indians living in straw huts. Some of these people, including women and children, were bathing in a river naked as jay birds. One of my friends said that I was driving too fast, but my missionary upbringing said that I should step on the gas. One other interesting thing we experienced was multi-colored bananas on a road-side stand. They were selling green, red and yellow bananas. We also saw bright colored birds that looked like parakeets flying through the trees. Our decision to return on this mountainous and winding road was well worth the extra time we spent driving it. When we got back to Laredo, we became aware that time was running out on our summer break. We decided on one more thing that would enable us to claim that our trip covered three countries. We headed northeast towards Detroit, Michigan. There, we crossed into Ontario, Canada, briefly visiting Niagara Falls, and finally arriving back in New York City. On this grand adventure, we had driven a total of 12,500 miles. This distance is equivalent to about ½ the circumference of the Earth. That is a real accomplishment for three young men traveling in a 1934 Chevrolet.

A final and startling footnote to this story: It was reported that later on in 1947, Mt. Popocatepetl had started to get active again. What a show we missed! I graduated from Duke University on June, 1949, with a Bachelor of Science in Electrical Engineering degree. There were no further adventures!

figure 5.9 [23]

DUKE CHAPEL

DUKE UNIVERSITY---DURHAM, N. CAROLINA

CHAPTER 6

THE DAWN OF HIGH FIDELITY RECORDING

The year was 1948. The first long playing vinyl record was being introduced to the music world by Columbia Records. This was before my graduation from Duke University in 1949. One afternoon, word was going around the university campus that Columbia Record engineers were going to have a demonstration of a new type of record. I rushed to the engineering lab and I listened in wonderment to the sound of music coming from a 10-inch vinyl disc rotating at a very slow speed, which I found out later, was 33 & 1/3 RPM. I had been brought up on 78 RPM record speeds, so listening to the sound emanating from such a slow moving record was absolutely magical. I was witnessing the dawn of the LP record. Move forward to the early 50's. I was still a bachelor with little of life's worries. At that time, I had two engineering buddies who shared a common interest in high fidelity music reproduction. Since the introduction of the 10-inch LP record by Columbia, the recording industry had evolved and had begun to produce a 12-inch LP record, which would soon become the standard of the recording industry. The 12-inch record was being used primarily to record classical and Broadway Shows music. My two buddies and I were enthusiastically embracing this new audio dimension.

During this time, I heard that the National Symphony Orchestra was going to have a historic concert in Constitution Hall, Washington D.C. We agreed to buy tickets and attend this event. When we found our seats, we were surprised to look down on an empty stage. Against the back of the platform were several of the largest speakers I had ever seen. I estimated their height to be at least 6 to 8 ft.. Usually, by this time, members of the orchestra would be seated, warming up their instruments. As we waited, a small group of flute and clarinet players walked in and started practicing. A short while later, they were joined by a larger group who began playing their 'cellos. The next group to enter was the violins, followed by the brass section, and finally the base and percussion musicians. After a short warm-up period, the conductor came to the podium, and the concert got underway. Towards the end of the first half, an unusual event took place. We noticed that the violinists weren't actually playing their instruments, but were holding their bows in mid-air. The other members of the orchestra were also in a suspended state of animation. The amazing thing, however, was that the symphony we had been listening to never lost a note. The sound was emanating from the huge speakers, without any degradation in volume or quality. Soon thereafter, the orchestra resumed playing without missing a beat! When the first half of the concert ended, the audience was told that someone by the name of Avery Fischer had set up LP recordings of the concert, and had synchronized them perfectly with the live music of the orchestra. What a wonderful demonstration of high fidelity music reproduction. After the concert, the three of us had to meet the man behind this electronic marvel. We met Mr. Fisher and complimented him on his musical feat.

Now I have to digress from this event and turn back several months. The three of us had heard that the Washington, D.C. transportation system had put up for sale FM receivers that were installed in the nation's capital streetcars. The transit system had been piping in music to their street cars for the entertainment of their passengers. Unfortunately, they occasionally broke in with advertisements. This soon resulted in complaints from some of their customers that they were forced to listen to unwanted commercials. As a result of this uproar, the transit company removed all of the FM receivers from their streetcars and put them up for sale. I got wind of this and purchased one of them. Automobile radios at this time were only capable of receiving AM broadcasts. Stations broadcasting FM transmissions were, therefore not listened to in cars. I then came up with one of my rare brilliant ideas. Why not install my FM radio in my car, and see if it would receive the FM music being broadcast by several FM radio stations. After the installation, the three of us drove around town, (we lived in Baltimore, MD at the time), and were delighted to see that we were listening to beautiful FM music. We even drove through car tunnels without loss of signal. Evidently the overhead streetcar electric lines served as antennas. I'll now return to our meeting with Avery Fisher at the Washington concert. Mr. Fisher was already established as one of the country's leading manufacturers of high fidelity equipment. In fact, my pre-amplifier in my high fidelity music system had the Fisher label. He listened attentively to my discussion of our FM car experiment. We then asked him if he thought that FM car radios could be built. He quickly said that since FM transmissions were "line of sight", that this limited the use of FM radios in automobiles. That application would have to wait for future technical breakthroughs. It wasn't long after, that we learned that Fisher was coming out, for the first time, with FM radios for automobiles. I can only imagine what my future would have been if I had had the resources to put my idea into reality!

CHAPTER 7

THE COLD WAR WITH THE SOVIET UNION

The Start of My Engineering Career

The date was June, 1949. World War II had ended with the unconditional surrender of Japan four years earlier. I had just graduated from Duke University with a brand new engineering degree in my pocket. The world was mine to conquer! What I didn't realize was that I had graduated in a year that was later to be known as the engineering depression. What happened is that I, together with many thousands of veterans, had taken advantage of the G.I. Bill to obtain an education at government's expense. The U.S. economy was not in a healthy state, thus contributing to an over-abundance of engineers. Before graduation, I had experienced a hint of what lay ahead. I found out, during my senior year, that only the top 10% of Duke's graduating class had been offered an engineering job by all of the many American businesses that had sent recruiters to our school. Unfortunately, I wasn't in that group. What lay ahead for the country was two wars. One was the Korean War that started on June 25, 1950 and ended with an armistice on July 27, 1953. The other one, called "The Cold War", had as an antagonist the Soviet Union, and extended from 1946 to 1991. The latter one would dominate my life for my first ten years as an engineer. I spent several months sending out letters to many large companies, all to no avail. During this time, I was staying with my older sister Peggy, and her husband Ray, in their house in Jersey City, N.J. Totally discouraged over the job situation, I started to scan the want ads in the local newspaper. I ran across an ad by National Airlines at the nearby Newark International Airport. I immediately arranged for an interview, and was delighted to be offered a job as an Operations Agent. I had no idea what this position was all about, but I soon found out that the many responsibilities of an Operation Agent included the supervision of the loading of baggage and miscellaneous freight before each flight. This meant being sure that the total weight load was properly distributed on the aircraft, and did not exceed the maximum allowed. I also helped as a Ticket Agent at the front counter during peak rush periods. During this time, I continued my campaign of letters to a variety of corporations. After several months on my airport job, I was pleasantly surprised to receive two offers from two large companies. One was the Glen L. Martin aircraft company in Baltimore, MD., and the second one was the Air Arm Division of Westinghouse Electric located in Baltimore's Friendship Airport. The position at the Martin Co. was that of Associate Engineer, while Westinghouse offered me the position of Junior Engineer. I was impressed by the title of Associate Engineer, so I found myself flying down to Baltimore to interview with the Martin Co. I would later regret this decision. I then made a tactical mistake. I wrote a letter to Westinghouse advising them that I had accepted a job with another company. I did this before allowing sufficient time to determine if this had been the right decision.

Little did I know that I had not only made a big mistake, but that I would soon establish a new record at the Martin Co. My first day there started out with high promise. I spent the day visiting various departments to see where I would fit best. I told my engineer escort which department I was most interested in. To my great surprise, I was offered a position with the project I disliked the most. (Little did I know at the time that God had other plans for me.) I was told to report to my new manager, where I was confronted with my second disappointment. They didn't even have a desk for me, so I was forced to sit opposite my new manager at his desk. Noon came and I asked where the cafeteria was. He gave me some general directions, and I left with his parting words: "Lunch is only 30 minutes long. Be sure you are back on time". What I didn't realize was how large the company was. It wasn't long before I became hopelessly lost. As I wandered down the hallways, a group of three men saw me and came over to speak to me. One of the three was a youngish man with red hair. He quickly found out that I was newly hired. They immediately invited me to lunch with them. As we sat at the table, I unloaded on them my unhappiness with my new job, and the fact that I wasn't even given a desk to work at. My red-haired host wanted to know my manager's name. After we finished our meal, he offered to show me around the plant. I told him that my new manager's parting words were, as I left for lunch, to be sure to get back on time. My host said not to worry about it that he would take care of any problems with my manager. At that moment, I began to suspect that I was dealing with a person in higher authority. The tour of the plant, which included a visit to where they were assembling the giant P6M water-born jet bomber, called the "SeaMaster," took about two hours.

figure 7.1 [24]

The Martin P6M SeaMaster

(The P6M never entered active service. The nuclear submarine took its place)

My escort walked me back to my engineering section, and again told me not to worry about my tardiness, that he would take care of any problems.

When I got back to my manager's desk, he didn't say a word, but kept looking at some paperwork on his desk. After several minutes had passed, he suddenly looked up and asked: "Who did you have lunch with?" I told him about my red-haired friend. He didn't say a word for a long time, and then he finally looked up and said that my friendly host was the Engineering Department General Manager. After another long moment of silence, he looked up at me and said "Barnes, this isn't going to start things right with me". I didn't answer him, and continued to read some documents he had previously given to me. The next day, history repeated itself and I once again got lost looking for the lunch room. This time, however, I was able to finally find it on my own. And so went my second unhappy day. On the 3rd day, I came to the conclusion that I had made a bad choice between the two jobs I had been offered. At lunch time, I located an outside phone and called the Westinghouse employment office. I quickly told them about my Martin Co. experience, and asked whether the job I had been previously offered was still open. They immediately said yes, and invited me to come down for an interview. What a relief! I never returned to the Martin Co. Later on that week I mailed my badge back to them. Two weeks later, to my great surprise, I received a check covering two weeks work. Actually, of course, I had only worked 2 and ½ days there. I had probably established an all-time record at the Martin Co. for the employment of a professional employee. This story has an unusual ending. Six months had passed. At that time, I belonged to an engineering society called the "American Institute of Electrical Engineers".

I received an invitation to attend a special meeting of the society. The guest speaker was a scientist by the name of Werner Von Braun. To those not familiar with the birth of the American Space Program, Von Braun would ultimately become one of the great men in our Moon Program. After World War II, where he was a renowned rocket scientist in Germany, he was brought back to the States by our government. Even though von Braun was a key member of a German rocket team that designed the V-2 rocket that rained down on London during World War II, he brought with him invaluable experience in space rockets. The time was the early 50's and Von Braun had not yet achieved the notoriety that would await him 10 years later.

figure 7.2 [25]

THE ROCKET SCIENTIST, WERNER VON BRAUN

During this period in his life, he was dedicated to being a "Space Salesman". He then presented to his audience of young engineers his design of a rocket capable of reaching the moon. It would be a four-stage monster rocket that would utilize a very large number of a relatively modest rocket he had previously designed. During intermission, another engineer approached me and asked: "Isn't your name Barnes?" I answered in the affirmative. Then he asked: "What ever happened to you?" It turned out that he had remembered me from the 3 days I had spent working at The Martin Co. He then gave me some surprising news. Six months after I abruptly left the company, my supervisor that had started me on a terrible first week, was fired. Fate has strange twists and turns, because I then established what I consider a very productive career at Westinghouse, and there was where I would later meet Phiddy, to whom I was married for 32 years. A final note: Ten years later, I joined a very small engineering group in Houston as an aerospace engineer on the Apollo Moon Program. Could Von Braun's presentation that day in the early 50's have provided me with a glimpse of what would ultimately become one of the highlights of my engineering career?

THE UNITED STATES DEFENSE PROGRAM

When I started work at the Air Arm Division of Westinghouse Electric, I had the position of Junior Engineer. That is the equivalent to an Apprentice Seaman in the navy. (The following narrative has unavoidable technical language which some readers may fine difficult to understand. This, however, covered a 10-year period during which I matured as a project engineer, and ultimately, many years afterward opened a door that would lead me into our country's Space Program).

Westinghouse had received a contract from the U.S. Air Force for the development of a target seeker known as the AN/DPN-34 radar. This radar was to be installed in the nose of a surface-to-air pilotless interceptor known as BOMARC. The interceptor was being built by the Boeing Co., together with Marquart Corp., and carried a nuclear device in the nose. It was part of a continental defense system known as SAGE. (This acronym stood for : "Semi-Automatic Ground Environment"). At that time in the 50's, the cold war with the Soviet Union was going full swing. A lot of people thought that it could become a hot war at any moment. Our Defense Dept. was concerned that a fleet of Russian bombers with nuclear bombs could fly over the Arctic region and destroy our cities on the East coast, killing millions of people. The BOMARC interceptor was capable of flying 300-400 miles offshore, and with its nuclear device, essentially wipe out a whole fleet of Russian bombers. It should be remembered that by this time, Russia had developed the hydrogen bomb. Armageddon was at our doorstep.

The AN/DPN-34 radar was designed to automatically track its target until the BOMARC warhead would destroy it. I would ultimately be involved in the highly classified world of electronic warfare. In a combat environment, enemy electronic systems would try to jam our target seeker before our nuclear device was activated. To counter this action, our radar would have to have anti-jam capabilities.

figure 7.3 [26]

THE SUPERSONIC BOMARC

In this electronic warfare world, this is called counter-counter measures. This secret environment, totally unknown to the public, would be where I would work for the next 10 years. Ultimately, I would have under my control a small fleet of military aircraft. My first assignment at Westinghouse, however, would be a very modest one. I was given the engineering job that no one, in our design department, wanted. The job consisted of designing and testing the interconnecting cable system that would tie the whole radar system together. As menial as this tasked appeared to the outsider, it provided me with unique knowledge. I was the only one who knew how the whole system tied together. The Good Lord above knew that this job was opening a door that would ultimately lead me to the position of project engineer. This is a prime example of starting with a very humble task that would lead me into an unbelievable set of experiences. What I will be describing in this chapter is nothing but amazing. To mention a few events that awaited me, they included the following: (1) The development and purchase of the first video tape recorder ever sold in this country; (2) The control of my own Air Force; (3) Assisting in the development of sophisticated electronic counter-countermeasures; and finally (4) an encounter with a Russian prime minister.

As the AN/DPN–34 radar was being completed by our design department, the planning for the next program, system's testing, started to take place. My knowledge of how the radar system interconnected opened the door to a career as a systems test engineer. This position would develop over the next few years to that of a project engineer with its large responsibilities and freedom from close supervision.

One of the most guarded secrets in developing a military radar system is its vulnerability to countermeasures from unfriendly sources. There are two types of countermeasures, passive and active. The most commonly used in the past was developed during World War II simultaneously by both Germany and the Allies. It was called "chaff", and is comprised of small strips of aluminum foil that are used to fool radars in thinking that it had acquired a target. Both sides in the war were trying to cover up the fact that they were using chaff. Active countermeasures uses electronic devices that emit a broad band of frequencies to completely blank out any radar that was targeting them. This type of radar jamming is the one that is currently used the most.

My initial assignment as a project engineer was to locate a site, preferably overlooking a large body of water, that could be used as a test site that would enable us to evaluate the capability of our radar system to operate against these countermeasures. Taking my right-hand engineer and my number one technician, we took off early one day on our scouting trip. The obvious choice was somewhere on the shoreline of Chesapeake Bay, which was reasonably close to our home plant. We looked and looked at sites on the western side of the bay, but found most areas populated with too many homes. We then approached the Chesapeake Bay Bridge which crossed over to a place called Kent Island on the eastern shore of Maryland. We found a small road that headed south that followed the beach line. Not very far down from the bridge was a small cleared area that was exactly what we were looking for.

figure 7.4 [27]

THE CHESAPEAKE BAY BRIDGE

A long story short—I found myself accomplishing the following tasks having had no former experience to guide me:

- Searching for the state agency that had the authority to approve the use of a small piece of public land.

- Arranging for a contractor to build a barbed-wire enclosure, a small guardhouse, a large wooden platform that we could use to mount our radar antenna, & flood lights to illuminate the entire area at night.

- Since this site had a government security classification of "Secret", we had to hire security guards to secure our site from any unwanted intruders They were provided with radio communications and weapons to guard our site 24/7.

- Purchasing a large semi-trailer to serve as our electronics lab, housing both radar components and instrumentation.

- Obtaining a large gasoline-driven electric generator to provide the site with electric power. This proved to be one of our biggest challenges. We finally obtained, with a big assist from the U.S. Air Force, one of the generators used to provide power to their large KC-135 jet transports when they were on the ground.

- Then we were confronted with another big challenge. We needed to get a large gasoline tank similar to those used in service stations. For safety reasons, we got digging equipment to place the tank underground.

All this work was accomplished in three months. The only thing left was to select personnel, both engineers and technicians, plus armed guards to man our test site. I don't mind saying that I, together with my crew, were very pleased with our accomplishments. I might add that back at home base, Westinghouse management, together with the maintenance department, provided all the support we needed. During all these preparations, I was working on test plans for use after activation of the test site. All I needed was the availability of government countermeasures systems. To accomplish our test program, I was provided with a liaison at Wright-Patterson Air Force Base. My contact was a captain that had the uncanny ability to obtain the use of anything we needed to accomplish our tasks. Our test objective was to simulate, as closely as possible, an encounter between an aircraft equipped with counter-measures and our radar system. Wright-Patterson, through our capable liaison captain, provided us with the following aircraft for us to use during our Kent Island test program. (I would, in the future, like to tell my family and friends that I had my own air force):

figure 7.5 [28]

BOEING KC-135 STRATOTANKER

- KC-135 Stratotanker
- Boeing developed this aircraft, simultaneously with the 707 Jet Airliner, from the same prototype. It became the first jet-powered refueling tanker. It was developed in the early 50's, and during the Cold War, a KC-135 was equipped with sophisticated counter-measures to be used in developing counter-countermeasures for many of the U.S.'s radars. A brief word of explanation. Counter-measures is a system that defended an aircraft from enemy fire. Counter-countermeasures was an opposing system designed to neutralize the other party's defense system. Since the Bomarc program had a very high priority, I, through my Wright-Patterson liaison, was able to obtain the use of a KC-135 in tests of Westinghouse's AN/DPN-34 target seeker.

figure 7.6 [29]

BOEING B-50 SUPERFORTRESS

- B-50 Superfortress
- This aircraft was a post World War II upgrade of the famous B-29 Superfortress used to carry the world's first atomic bombs dropped on Hiroshima & Nagasaki, Japan. The B-50 we used for our ground-to-air flight tests was equipped with sophisticated electronic counter-measures, and was more readily available than the KC-135.

figure 7.7 [30]

BOEING B-47 STRATOJET

- B-47 Stratojet
- The Boeing B-47 Stratojet had swept back wings, with six jet engines hanging under the wings. It was a long range medium bomber designed primarily to drop nuclear bombs on Russia in the event the Cold War turned into a hot war. It first flew on Dec. 17, 1947 and had a long 30-year career with the Air Force. The B-47 provided to us by Wright-Patterson had chaff dispensers, so we used it primarily to test the effectiveness of this type of passive counter-measures. I might add that our radar had problems with operating against chaff. Fortunately, a pulse-doppler radar was being developed that could completely neutralize the effectiveness of chaff. This new radar, called the AN/DPN-53 target seeker would not appear until we had concluded our Kent Island tests.

figure 7.8 [31]

AERO COMMANDER

- Aero Commander
- This was a twin-engine propeller driven aircraft built as a small passenger airplane. We used it as a target during our tests. At this time, I would like to add a historical note. The Aero Commander became the presidential transport for President Dwight Eisenhower between 1956 and 1960. It thus became the smallest "Air Force One" ever used as the President's plane, and also the first aircraft to have the now-familiar blue and white design.

figure 7.9 [32]

REPUBLIC F-105D THUNDERCHIEF

- Republic F-105 Thunderchief
- The F-105 was a supersonic fighter-bomber first flown in 1955, and capable of flying at Mach 2. It formally entered the service in 1958. Interestingly, this aircraft carried a greater bomb load than the B-17's used in World War II. During the late 60's and 70's, it would see major service in the Vietnam War. We used F-105's stationed at McGuire Air Force Base in southern New Jersey as target aircraft.

Now that I had "my" air force ready and willing, I started scheduling a series of ground-to-air tests at the Kent Island Test Site. All I had to do to obtain the use of one of the aircraft described above was to contact my Wright-Patterson liaison captain and make my requests known. Because of the high priority the AN/DPN-34 radar had, my requests were always honored. During these tests, design engineers from Westinghouse Air Arm Division would come to the site to observe and analyze the AN-DPN/34 radar system's performance in a real-time counter-measures environment. I will relate just a few unusual events that took place during these tests.

An encounter with Russia's Premier

In 1959, Vice President Nixon visited the Soviet Union. During this visit, he and Premier Krushchev, had an impassioned discussion on the merits of Russia's and the U.S.'s economic systems. The discussion took place at a model kitchen exhibit in Moscow. This became known as "The Great Kitchen Debate". Out of this meeting came an invitation by Vice President Nixon to Krushchev to visit the U.S. This would be the first visit by a Soviet Premier to the U.S. Krushchev brought his wife Nina and adult children. Little did I know that during this visit, I would have an encounter with the Russian Prime Minister that almost caused an international incident. It was September 1959. I was busy directing, by radio, the B-50 aircraft in making several runs on our Kent Island test site. While the B-50 was operating full-blast their electronic noise jammers, at that moment, Krushchev and family were heading south from New York City to Andrews Air Force Base near Washington, D.C. where they would be met by President Eisenhower. Suddenly, right in the middle of my test runs, the B-50 pilot abruptly came on the air and said that he would immediately have to stop the tests. I told him that I wasn't finished with the day's run, but he said that he couldn't talk to me and to call the next day. What had happened was that the B-50's countermeasures systems were filling the airways with electronic noise, interfering with Andrew's radars, and possibly endangering the incoming Russian aircraft. Needless to say, nothing was ever said about this incident. Since our tests had a "Secret" classification, this story was not reported by the media.

Encounter with duck hunters

On this particular day, we scheduled "Chaff" tests using our B-47 bomber. One of our tests was flown starting at 5000 ft. in altitude over "The Thomas Point Shoal" lighthouse on Chesapeake Bay across from Annapolis, MD, and descending to 500 ft. over our test site. This run was nicknamed "The Gun Barrel Run". It was a big favorite of the Air Force pilots who loved to use their big airplanes as a dive bomber. We had scheduled a "chaff" run not realizing that we were going to cause a major public relations incident. Not far from our test site were several duck blinds. On this day, some duck hunters were waiting inside their duck blinds, hoping that a passing duck might spot their duck decoys floating in the water. We didn't know these men were there, or we would have had our guards tell them that they had to leave for safety reasons. As our B-47 descended toward our site, they released a large cloud of chaff, which completely covered the water where the hunters were. Their hunting day was ruined! They immediately got out of their blind and stood on their nearby boat shaking their fists at us. That was the last time we conducted that kind of test run.

The B-50 Dare Devils

On this day, we scheduled several runs using our B-50 and its noise jammers. Toward the end of the test day, the flight crew requested one final "gun barrel" run. Word had gotten out at Wright-Patterson about this particular run. As they descended toward our test site, we became alarmed when the B-50 looked like it was flying too low. As it turned out, they came down to about 200 ft. above us before they pulled up. The backwash from the plane shook up our radar trailer, knocking off supplies from off the shelves. I immediately radioed up, asking them what in the world were they doing. Without a word they headed back to home base. That night I had a bad dream where I saw our B-50 flying down toward our site, then abruptly banking to the left to avoid the Chesapeake Bay Bridge, before falling into the bay. That was the last time that I scheduled a "gun barrel" run!

figure 7.10 [33]

THOMAS POINT LIGHTHOUSE

THE STORY OF THE VIDEO TAPE RECORDER

The year was 1954. The ground-to-air tests at the Kent Island test site were well underway. One day, I happened to be perusing an issue of "TIME" magazine, when towards the back, in a section on new technologies, a small article caught my attention. It described the development of video tape recorders. Magnetic tape audio recorders had been around for several years, but a commercially available video tape recorder was still in early stages of development. The "TIME" article indicated there were three companies working on a video tape recorder (VTR). When I read the article, I had a brilliant idea. What if I contracted for a VTR, and then installed both the recorder and the BOMARC radar in an aircraft capable of high altitude flight? A series of flights could then be made against both passive and electronic countermeasures, then record the output of the radar to be played in laboratory design tests over and over again. This could result in considerable savings in reducing the number of expensive aircraft flights. The "TIME" magazine article identified the following three companies working on developing a video tape recorder:

(1) RCA/Camden, N.J.

(2) AMPEX Corp.

(3) Bing Crosby Enterprises

My manager gave me the go-ahead to pursue this idea. I started by writing letters to all three companies explaining my plan to install the VTR in an aircraft to record radar video for later use in a design laboratory. I received the following responses:

(1) RCA: Not interested at this time. The VTR they were developing filled a whole room.

(2) AMPEX: No response

(3) Bing Crosby Enterprises (BCE): I immediately received an invitation to visit their lab in Los Angeles, California and discuss what we were looking for. I readily accepted, and when I got to Los Angeles, I was royally treated by their entire engineering department.

At this time, I should provide some background information on the history of the video tape recorder. Bing Crosby Enterprises (BCE) gave the world's first demonstration of video tape recording (VTR), in Los Angeles on November 11, 1951. Two people, John T. Mullin and Wayne R. Johnson had been working to develop a VTR since 1950. The quality of the video wasn't very good, but it was a start. By October 1952, Wayne Johnson had improved the quality of the recorded video to the point that on October 3, 1952 he proclaimed the first high resolution motion picture ever produced by means other than photography. It should be noted, at this time, that the BOMARC Air Defense System I was working on was classified "Secret". The national defense of our country was of major concern, for many thought we were threatened by Russia's nuclear arsenal. What this meant, was, there would be no media coverage of what we were doing. The only exception to this, and the only public information in national media available to even hint at the existence of this project, was an article that appeared in "Billboard" magazine, Hollywood, California, on October 2, 1954 stating that Bing Crosby Enterprises (BCE) had been awarded the first contract ever for a television taping machine by the Air Arm Division of Westinghouse Electric in Baltimore, MD. (Note: The word "Television" is in error. As stated above, the real purpose of the video tape recorder was to support a classified government program involving countermeasures. This purpose could not, obviously, be divulged in the "Billboard" article). "Billboard" went on to quote that the Executive Director of the Crosby Electronics Division hoped that the government order would hasten commercial acceptance of video tape recording. Through this contract with Bing Crosby Enterprises, I would be able to say that I was instrumental in the development and purchase of the first video tape recorder (VTR), and I might add the first airborne VTR, commercially sold in the U.S. Total cost of this recorder was $175,000. The year was 1954. AMPEX, who was also working on video tape recording techniques, would later claim to have developed and released, in 1956, the first commercially successful VTR. We beat that by two years!

While all this was going on, I communicated with my Wright-Patterson liaison that I needed an aircraft capable of high altitudes to serve as my radar plane. He told me that the United Kingdom was developing a light bomber called the "Canberra" which was capable of reaching high altitudes, up to 45,000 ft. The U.S. was also, at this time, interested in an aircraft that could serve both as a bomber and as a reconnaissance plane. The British supplied us with seven prototypes of this aircraft.

figure 7.11 [34]

THE FIRST VIDEO TAPE RECORDER SOLD IN THE UNITED STATES

(OCT. 1954)

(Note: I'm on the left. The airborne unit was the center panel with the two reels)

ENGINEERING

Scanner

AIR ⊙ ARM

BALTIMORE   MARYLAND

Vol. 4 No. 8   *MARCH 18, 1955*

FIRST AIRBORNE VIDEO TAPE RECORDER BUILT

Al Barnes, Missile Systems Section, engineer in charge of the recorder, and Dan Licht, his assistant, testing the gadget. In the left rack, top down, the units are cycle unit, tape transport mechanism (removable for airborne use), capstan power amplifier and the 400 cycle power supply. The right rack contains the regulated power supply, two equalizer preamplifiers, channel selector output panel and three regulated power supplies. On the floor, behind Dan, are the airborne units: recording electronics chassis and recording electronics power supply. Al is holding the remote control box. A recent contract was issued to extend the frequency response range down from the present 20KC — 2 MC, to 5 CPS — 2 MC.

figure 7.12 [35]

Working On The Video Recorder With My No.1 Technician

figure 7.13 [36]

MARTIN B57A BOMBER

I, or should I say, my Air Force liaison, was fortunate to obtain the use of one of these seven aircraft. The U.S. Air Force changed its designation from "Canberra" to B-57. On arrival at Friendship Airport in Baltimore, MD, Westinghouse personnel began installing the AN/DPN-34 target seeker into the B-57. In the meantime, I was making several trips to the Crosby Electronics Lab to follow up on the video tape recorder we had ordered. It was finally delivered and also installed in the B-57. An article would later appear (1958), in Westinghouse's publication "Westinghouse Engineer" attesting to the fact that our VTR was the first video tape recorder sold commercially in the U.S. The article further describes the pioneering use of the recorder in the development of air defense radars. Needless to say, I was very proud of this accomplishment. Someone told me later that my video tape recorder ended up in "The Smithsonian Museum" in Washington D.C. I have never been able to confirm if this is true. Perhaps on a future trip to the nation's capital, I'll have a chance to see my recorder.

CHAPTER 8

THE APOLLO MOON PROGRAM

I Join The Space Program.

The year is 1962. My job at Westinghouse was coming to an end. President Kennedy had presented a major challenge to our country. He wanted the Space Agency (NASA) to develop the hardware that would take man to the moon and return him safely back to Earth within a decade. In a speech to a joint session of Congress on May 25, 1961, he presented the daring space project. It would be called "The Apollo Moon Program". He repeated the challenge in a famous speech he made at Rice University in Houston, Texas in September 1962. For 10 years, I had been working at Westinghouse on a defense system that was designed to blow up people in one atomic blast. Even though I was proud to have contributed to this very necessary and critical program, I yearned for a new challenge in some peaceful non-military endeavor. President Kennedy's moon program was just what I was looking for. The big question, however, was how to get on this new program. I then heard that General Electric had received a contract to not only build the pre-launch checkout system, but also to support NASA management in the area of reliability and quality engineering.

The only opening G.E. had at that time was in the very area I had been working on at Westinghouse, namely the S.A.G.E air defense program. My new destination was Syracuse, New York. I had been working there for a short six months, when I heard the exciting news that a small group of G.E. supervisors were visiting our plant to interview for positions in the newly created Apollo Support Department located in Houston, Texas. Afraid of receiving a turn-down, I decided not to let my current manager know of my intention to get an interview with our visitors. This could have placed my present job in jeopardy, but I was willing to take the chance. With guidance from the Good Lord, this turned out to be the most important decision I would make in my entire engineering career. It was a life-changing moment. The next week, I was on my way flying to Houston, Texas for an interview. During the long flight to Texas, I perused an aviation industry magazine called "Aviation Weekly". There happened to be a feature article in the magazine about the Apollo Program. In the article, it mentioned that NASA was going to decentralize its structure, and give semi-autonomous management control to the ten operational centers. The NASA headquarters center in Washington, D.C. was to provide overall guidance and direction for the agency. G.E. with its responsibility for development of the Apollo check-out system was headquartered in Daytona Beach, Florida. Most employees involved with the Apollo Program were attached to the Daytona Beach operation. I was told by other engineers, that the Florida location offered the best future. I then read in the aviation magazine that Houston, Texas would be the home for the astronaut corps, and also be the location for the all-important mission control center. I decided to aim for employment in the Houston operations, as this location appeared to have the best future opportunities. NASA-Houston at the time was operating out of several rented buildings. The Manned Spacecraft Center, (later re-named "The Johnson Space Center") was being built in the Clear Lake area south of Houston. When I called on the interviewing G.E. managers, I was told to go to a Holiday Inn located across from one of NASA's leased office buildings. To my surprise, G.E. Houston Operations was working out of five rooms at the Inn. The handful of employees were mostly in management. I was offered a position as Reliability Engineer, and was told that the G.E. Apollo Support Operation would grow to 90 employees. This number was way off, as the G.E. Center actually grew to 1100 employees. For the next few years, I advanced in my responsibilities to the point that I was promoted to the position of Manager of the Reliability Test Engineering unit. I started out with only a secretary and 2 temporary employees. I had to interview and hire one dozen experienced test engineers. They would ultimately be assigned to each of the Apollo spacecraft, including the one that would be the first to land on the moon. This historic spacecraft would be called Apollo 11. The Apollo spacecraft was comprised of a Command Module, a Service Module, and a Lunar Module. The Command Module contained the flight crew, together with life support and all the necessary command and control systems. The Service Module provided propulsion, fuel and oxygen tanks. The Lunar Module was the part of the spacecraft that landed on the surface of the Moon. My engineers served as reliability project engineers providing overall surveillance of all the tests of the spacecraft subsystems. For the next five years from 1962 to 1967, most of NASA's efforts were concentrated on developing and testing Apollo's hardware.

figure 8.1 [37]

THE APOLLO COMMAND/SERVICE MODULE

figure 8.2 [38]

THE APOLLO LUNAR MODULE

figure 8.3 [39]

SATURN V – APOLLO MOON ROCKET

figure 8.4 [40]

APOLLO 11 FLIGHT CREW (1st LUNAR LANDING)

(ARMSTRONG, COLLINS, ALDREN)

Albert E. Barnes

The Death of Four Astronauts

The year was 1967, and it would turn out to be one of the worst years in NASA's early history. A Command Module designated as Spacecraft 12, (and later changed to Apollo 1), was being prepared for transfer from the manufacturer to the Kennedy Space Center (KSC). Crucial ground tests would be run involving three astronauts, and was designed to simulate actual space-flight conditions. There would be some events, however, that would contribute either directly or indirectly to what would end up as a major tragedy. The company that I worked for, G.E., was responsible for identifying combustible materials in the Command Module. As the G.E. engineer responsible for the inspection red-tagged hazardous materials to be removed, he was informed that these items would be attended to when the spacecraft arrived at KSC. In a post-accident investigation, it was determined that Dr. Joe Shea, the Apollo Program Manager, had asked the spacecraft manufacturer, North American Aviation, to take care of the issue of flammable materials. Unfortunately, in order to meet test schedules, this matter apparently was not taken care of properly. A second event involved the manufacturer of the environmental control system. During tests at their facility where they were using 100% oxygen, a fire broke out that seriously damaged the Apollo test hardware. There is no record that this event was transmitted directly to the personnel conducting the tests on Spacecraft 012. The third event involved one of the three astronauts, Gus Grissom. Gus had been complaining about problems with the spacecraft trainer that simulated the operation in the cabin environment. He had developed serious doubts about the integrity of Spacecraft 012. Sensing, or perhaps having an intuitive glimpse of what was about to happen to him and his other two companion astronauts, Gus had been trying to convince NASA management to install three fire extinguishers in the spacecraft's cabin. All to no avail. In desperation, he wrote a letter to G.E. management, pleading that they try to convince their NASA counterparts to agree to the installation of the fire extinguishers. The letter never saw the light of day, and no action was ever taken. Whether this would have helped during a rapid oxygen-fed fire is highly questionable. The final fatal step, was NASA's decision to simulate flight conditions, and pressurize the cabin with 100% pure oxygen above the normal sea-level atmospheric pressure. This created a bomb waiting to go off. Any spark would be a disaster, and that is exactly what happened, because at 6:30 P.M. on January 27, a major fire erupted in the Apollo spacecraft, and in a few minutes, the three astronauts (Gus Grissom, Ed White, and Roger Chaffee) were killed. In a subsequent trip to KSC, I had the opportunity to see the inside of the burned-out Command Module. Death must have come quickly to the three men because the interior was just a pile of ashes. Before the fatal tests, and after an acceptance test review, the three astronauts gave Dr. Joe Shea, the Apollo Program Manager, a picture of the spacecraft, with the heads of the 3 astronauts bowed in prayer. The inscription on the photo read "It isn't that we don't trust you, Joe, but this time we've decided to go over your head".

At the beginning of this story, I labeled the section "The Death of 4 Astronauts". Although not generally known to the public, 5 other Apollo astronauts, in addition to the 3 that were killed by the fire, were killed in accidents. I added one of these to my story about the 3 at KFC, because it was a strange story that nobody, to my knowledge, has told. My wife Phiddy and I were neighbors of Marj and Deke Slayton.

figure 8.5 [41]

DEKE SLAYTON, APOLLO CHIEF ASTRONAUT

(A DEAR PERSONAL FRIEND)

Deke was head of the Apollo astronaut corps, and was responsible for assigning the original seven astronauts to each of the first Apollo missions. Phiddy decided to invite the Slayton's to dinner. We had also invited the G.E. Houston Operations manager as a "Get acquainted" gesture. The date was June 6, 1967. This was a little over four months since the tragic fire at KSC. While we were seated chatting and having dinner, a telephone call came in for Deke. As he talked, a somber look came over his face. At the end of the call, he told us that something had come up, and that he would have to leave immediately. What we didn't know was that he was told that one of his astronauts had been killed in a car accident. His name was Edward Givens. It was reported that Givens had been attending a meeting of a fraternal organization south of Houston. He was returning at the wheel of his Volkswagen when he made a wrong turn that resulted in his death. I decided to drive out to see where the accident had occurred. I came up with the startling conclusion that a housing developer's road sign was the cause of the accident. I was very familiar with this area, since my wife and I lived in a small community called Friendswood, several miles east of the scene of the accident. Re-constructing the event, I drove south on a highway called "Telephone Rd", starting approximately where Givens final trip began. As I drove, I noticed a large sign on the right that had a big left turn arrow, advertising the developer's new sub-division in Friendswood. This sign was not placed before the road leading to Friendswood, but rather just before, at a secondary street on the left, one block away.

figure 8.6 [42]

ASTRONAUTS ED WHITE, GUS GRISSOM, ROGER CHAFFEE

figure 8.7 [43]

ASTRONAUT EDWARD GIVENS

Unfortunately, the street dead-ended 2 blocks later. Givens, totally unaware of this, drove his VW to the end of the street, where it went head-on into a ditch. He thought that, as the road sign indicated, he was to make a left turn to Friendswood on that first street. The sign was placed one street before he was supposed to turn. Edward Given's career ended as the result of miss-reading a developer's sign. He died on the way to a hospital. He was one of the first 19 astronauts selected by NASA in April, 1966. A final word: This story is not intended in any way to imply any responsibility on the part of the un-named developer for what occurred. After all is said and done, it was an accident.

I worked a total of fourteen years for General Electric in support of NASA's Manned Spacecraft Center, Houston Tx. During this time I was the Unit Manager over a group of approximately two dozen systems test engineers. There were many events during this period where I felt that I was making a contribution to our Nation's Space Flight Program. I don't want to, however, burden the reader with technical discussions that would appeal only to engineers. There is one more story that I will relate because it had such a large impact. During the aftermath of the Apollo fire at KSC, NASA assigned responsibility to a NASA manager to travel to the North American Aviation plant in California and determine if there were any management systems that could be improved in the manufacture of the re-designed Apollo spacecraft. The area that he found that appeared to have shortcomings was a management system called "Non-conformance Discrepancies", which is a fancy name for the reporting of failures. I undertook a trip to the North American Aviation plant and arranged for 3 to 4 young engineers to help in this investigation. Unfortunately, word of this effort got back to my G.E. manager who angrily asked "What in the world are you doing?" It turned out that I had stepped on his NASA's customer toes. My manager was providing direct support to the NASA manager responsible for reliability and quality engineering.

This turned out to be politically unfortunate because the NASA manager undertaking the program scrutiny at North American Aviation was working independently of the NASA managers G.E. was supporting in Houston. I quickly received a phone call from my manager, who told me to cease all my support efforts until further notice. I protested this vigorously until he barked the following into the phone: "You are to stop immediately your support activity. This is a direct order! I am not running a democracy!" He then hung up the phone. I stood there in disbelief since I and my group felt that what we were doing was making a major contribution toward the safety of the entire Apollo Program. I then held an impromptu meeting with my small group of engineers. They told me to do what I thought was best. After a brief moment, I told them to continue their work. I thought at the time that my engineering career at G.E. would come to an abrupt end. The end of this story was that nothing more was ever said to me about the incident, and NASA went on to totally change the failure reporting system at North American Aviation.

During my 14 years on the space program, I would travel many times to both North American Aviation in Los Angeles, and the Kennedy Space Center (KSC) in Florida. In the early 60's, NASA had started building the Apollo spacecraft at the North American plant in California. To assure the safety of the astronauts, NASA management planned to have two unmanned flights before any flights would be undertaken with flight crews. These early flights would be sub-orbital, which meant that they would leave the earth's atmosphere and after a short flight, they would re-enter without going into orbit. In support of these two flights, I had the privilege of preparing, for NASA management, a presentation that they would give at a pre-flight review at the Kennedy Space Center. During these reviews, I sat in a visitor's section overlooking large semi-circular tables where NASA program managers were seated preparing for the review. In the middle of the center space, a slide projector was set up to show the slides I had prepared. These slides covered significant failures that had occurred during testing of the Apollo hardware. The material used for the slides was obtained from NASA engineers responsible for overseeing the various subsystems being built at subcontractor's facilities. (At this point, I would like to say that a total of approximately 20,000 people were busy working on the Apollo Program throughout the United States). After the lights were turned down, and a NASA engineer started the slide presentation, an embarrassing event took place. The poor NASA employee had mixed up the order of the slides. With a signal from my manager, I stepped down to the projector and saved the day by quickly re-organizing the slides and then continuing by operating the slide projector. The time was now early 1971, and the United States had achieved the challenge made by John F. Kennedy almost 10 years before, of sending men to the moon and returning them safely within the decade.

One day, during my lunch hour in our home town of Nassau Bay, Texas, which was across from NASA's Manned Spacecraft Center, I was killing time looking at a collection of books on a book spinner. One particular book caught my attention. The name on the cover was "Doc Anderson, The Man Who Sees Tomorrow". I had never heard of him before, but he had made several startling predictions. These included predicting the death of major political figures, the development of the atomic bomb, the end of World War II, plus many others.

After reading all this, I decided that I had to find where Doc Anderson lived, and I would then get his phone number and would make an appointment to see him. In early 1971, I planned a trip to the Kennedy Space Center with a detour by way of Chattanooga, Tennessee where Doc lived. When I arrived there, I took a taxi and found myself at the doorstep of a quaint cottage, decorated with a Pennsylvania Dutch hex sign. I found Doc Anderson to be a very large man. In fact, before he became a well-known psychic, he had boxed in the ring as a prizefighter, starred as a wrestler, and was considered to be one of the world's leading experts on "Judo". Before I was taken to his office, I started to look at the many photographs of celebrities on his walls. Two of them caught my attention. I could not believe my eyes. One was a photograph of John Foster Dulles, who was the U.S. Secretary of State under President Dwight D. Eisenhower. You could have knocked me over with a feather. Dulles had become famous as a proponent of the theory of "Brinkmanship" and massive retaliation in dealing with unfriendly nations. This theory would take our country to the very brink of nuclear war. Nowadays, we would call this tactic a "Game of chicken". Hopefully, the other side would then back down. It seemed unbelievable that a person of this international stature would consult with a psychic. Perhaps he worried about this policy, and wanted to see if the world was going to blow up. Unfortunately, I don't remember what Secretary Dulles wrote on his autographed picture. Could it have been an inquiry about the possibility of a future atomic war with Soviet Russia? The second photograph I noticed was very familiar. It was a picture of astronaut John Glenn who had become famous by being the first American to orbit the earth on Feb. 20, 1962. In his handwriting on the photo he wrote "You were right Doc. Everything worked out OK". Obviously, Glenn had checked with Doc Anderson before he made his famous flight.

I mention these two photos to illustrate Doc Anderson's psychic abilities. As far as my interview went, there were only two noteworthy events. He predicted that in 5 or 6 years I would no longer work for a large company, but I would be free to be on my own. The reading took place in 1971. In late 1976, 5 years later, this became true because that year I chose to end my engineering career. From then on, I would be into my second life-time career, in sales. Since I had chosen outdoor sales, I was totally independent of any supervision, and I was pretty much on my own, relying primarily on commissions. I continued selling until I was able to open up my own business. The second noteworthy event during the interview was that he always saw me in a priest's clothing whenever he looked at me. Could this have been a past life? He ended the interview by telling me that he would meet me at the Chattanooga Airport if I should ever make an appointment to see him in the future. I thought that this was remarkable considering his national fame. Unfortunately, I never got to see him again. This story has a very sad ending. The year was 1980. A major rainfall had flooded Chattanooga. Doc Anderson was crossing what normally was a small stream. The water was much deeper than he thought and his car began to flood. He got out of the car, but was immediately swept away by the churning waters. The man who could see tomorrow apparently did not foresee his own death by drowning. Some people say he was not a true psychic because of this. His remarkable record of predictions, although not perfect, did not warn him about his own death. I have a possible explanation. If he had foreseen what was going to happen, he would surely try to avoid it. I don't believe that you can alter the future. I'll touch on this subject in a later chapter on pre-destination and free will.

CHAPTER 9

I START A NEW CAREER

The year was 1976, and the G.E. contract with NASA was coming to an end. I had been working as an engineer for approximately 25 years, and was now 50 years old. Ahead of me stretched 15 years before I reached the age where I could claim Social Security and Medicare. I now had two choices: One would be to start looking for an engineering job elsewhere, and the second one was to get out of engineering altogether. General Electric always considered the Houston Operations as an outpost, and there would be no automatic transfers to another G.E. plant. In fact, unlike the beginning of my career at G.E., I don't recall any visiting G.E. managers from any other plants coming to interview prospects in Houston. I then had to face the challenge of finding a new job, probably with another company. This time, however, there was another factor to consider, I was 50 years old! At that time, I made a major decision similar to the one I had made 15 years earlier to seek a job in the Space Program. I decided to seek a position in sales, where I would finally get free from the 8 to 5 restrictive office environment. There are basically two types of sales people: one would operate primarily as a retail salesperson, and the other would essentially be a free agent to come and go as he desired. The retail salesperson had the security of being a paid employee, whereas the outside salesman was on his own, relying primarily on commissions. The choice was simple. I wanted the freedom of the outside salesperson. I remembered President Reagan's famous words when he was asked if he felt like a salesman when presenting new ideas to the country. He said that half the world was in sales and half the world was prospective customers. A daunting thought crossed my mind. I had no sales experience. How was I, at the age of 50, going to get started, and with whom? My wife, Phiddy, suggested that I compose and ad wherein I would list what I thought were my strongest personal capabilities. The ad would not mention my engineering experience, but it would present what I thought were the reasons for my success in life. The thought of a generic ad that would ignore my 25 years in engineering, both as an individual contributor and as a manager, didn't turn me on, but I went along with the idea. The next problem was to place the ad in a publication that had a national audience. There were only 3 newspapers that came to mind, and they were: The New York Times, USA Today, and the Christian Science Monitor. My wife Phiddy was a member of the Christian Science Church, a church that I always thought was too far out of the mainstream, but which I learned to understand over the years. Then I thought, God's relationship to us is from individuals directly to Him. After all, I remember the famous words in the New Testament that were expressed when Jesus died on the cross. Matthew, Chapter 27, vs. 51 states that the veil of the temple was torn in two from top to bottom. There was no longer need for a priest to intercede for us. Everyone could appeal to God directly, irrespective of his church's affiliation. In other words, I wasn't to judge another one's belief, just because it didn't coincide with mine. And then a small miracle took place.

In faraway California, a man who incidentally was a Christian Scientist, was reading the Christian Science Monitor's ads and saw mine. Through coincidence, (which I call Divine Guidance), he happened to be looking for a salesman in Houston, TX. The position was for a salesman for The Paramount Greeting Card Company, out of Pawtucket, Road Island. That was the start of a 10-year career as a greeting card salesman. I would be given the responsibility for Paramount sales in East and South Texas. I would eventually end up as regional manager over 5 states, (Texas, New Mexico, Oklahoma, Arkansas, and Louisiana). At the end of my 10-year career with Paramount, I would receive a plaque stating that I had sold 1 million dollars' worth of greeting cards at wholesale. Not bad for an ex-aerospace engineer! This second career in sales would continue for 30 years! During this long period, I would sell, in addition to greeting cards, life insurance, advertising, and snack food services. The food service experience would ultimately blossom into a business of my own in 1991, which would continue for the following 20 years. We called our little business "Healthier Food Services" and we provided snacks to a great variety of small businesses, including banks, doctors, dentists, auto parts, etc. During this period, we opened up our business in 4 states. These states were Texas, Mississippi, Alabama, and Florida. Once we ran the business for 5 years, we would sell it at a good profit. We never operated more than one business at a time. My wife, Lovella, filled several jobs which included purchasing snack foods, packing the large snack boxes, and also taking care of the responsibilities of an office manager. I in turn, was the sole salesman and serviceman. This little business proved to be very successful. The largest one we owned operated out of Biloxi, Mississippi where we ended up with over 200 customers. My wife and I were no longer capable of handling the daily work, so we hired her sister, Freda Downs to help us. Honesty was absolutely essential in our little business, and we couldn't have found a more honest person than Freda. To this day, I am still operating a very small version of this food business. I am presently 85 years old, and I continually tell my wife that this little business keeps me healthy and active.

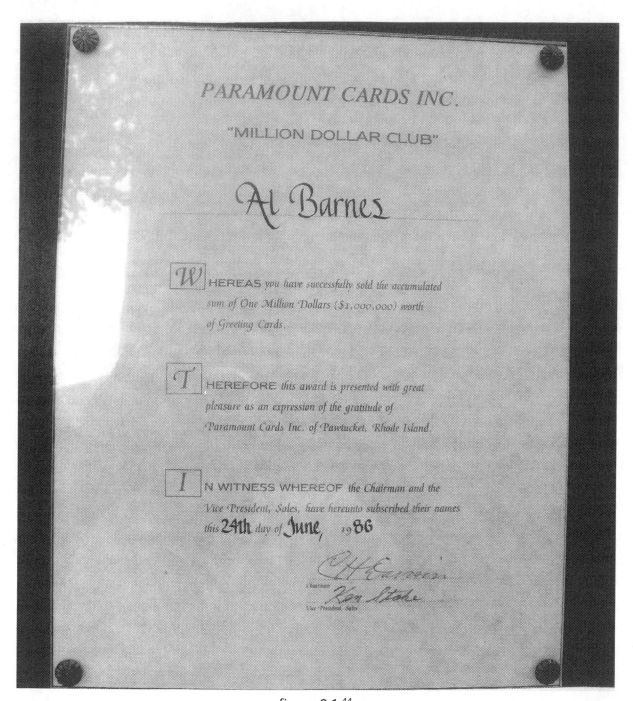

figure 9.1 [44]

MY MILLION DOLLAR SALES AWARD

PARAMOUNT GREETING CARDS

CHAPTER 10

DREAMS CAN PREDICT THE FUTURE

Everybody has dreams, however, what I am going to write about has no relationship to the attempt by psychologists to interpret everyday dreams. The dreams I am going to describe show that dreams can predict the future, both in real life experiences and in changes in one's life path. The year was 1967. A book had just been published called "The Sleeping Prophet". It was a book about the psychic Edgar Cayce. I heard a commercial about the book and I decided to purchase a copy. This was the beginning of an interest in the paranormal, i.e., psychic subjects. Ultimately, I joined a local Cayce study group. In this group, we discussed Edgar Cayce's predictions, together with his beliefs in interpreting a person's dreams. We were told the significance of dream symbols, such as dreams involving a house or an automobile. Cayce said that these symbols could represent our bodies, inasmuch as we live and move around in our bodies.

During this period, I made a concerted effort to remember my dreams. I was told to say loudly, three times, before I fell asleep: "I am going to remember my dreams when I awake"! I also kept a note pad and pen on my night stand to write down dreams as soon as I woke up. I started to get dreams that predicted future personal experiences. Specifically, these included several incidents that involved having emotional arguments with my late wife, Phiddy. The following are a few examples:

1. In this dream, I had a very big argument with Phiddy. After a heated exchange, she went to our bedroom closet and threw out all my clothes on the driveway. She then furiously took off in her car. I immediately got in my car to follow her, but found myself driving over rough roads. Ultimately, I caught up with her. Interpretation: She threatened to leave me. I would be able to catch up with her, but I would be going through some rough times before I did. Sure enough, a few days later we had a big argument. Happily, we were able to iron out our differences.

2. Phiddy and I lived for a short while in a house overlooking a bay near Galveston, Texas. One night, I dreamed that I saw two people in a small boat being tossed around by large waves. Cayce said that water many times represented human emotions. As I watched this scene, I found myself saying: "Don't give up! Keep paddling!" A few days later, we had another heated argument. Fortunately, again, it had a happy ending. Even though it isn't uncommon for spouses to argue, the two of us rarely had a big shouting match. At this time, I want to reassure the reader that Phiddy and I remained happily married for 32 years before she suddenly passed away in 1987.

Another more dramatic dream that predicted the future happened one night in the year 1975. In this dream, I saw myself in the family living room. On one side of the room was my mother standing by a dresser. On the dresser were three of the most beautiful watches one could ever imagine. They sparkled with a brilliant light. Across from her, I sat on a chair. To my left sat my older brother Sam, and to my right sat my niece Linda, who I always felt was more like a daughter than a niece. Linda was the oldest daughter of my oldest sister, Peggy, and her husband Ray. To the right side of the room was a large bay window. I saw mother go to the dresser, pick up one of the watches and then come around and give it to me. I was dazzled by its beauty. She then went back to the dresser, picked up a second watch and walked over to give it to me. She repeated this with a third watch. I then asked her why she didn't give one to my brother Sam. At that moment, I heard a loud noise.

My niece Linda then spoke and said that a big storm was coming. As soon as she said this, a large wave broke through the bay window and swept down the middle of the room, separating my brother Sam from the rest of us. This was my interpretation of the dream: The living room represented our family circle. Mother represented the one who bore us and thus gave us life. The watches represented time in our life experiences. The storm indicated a major emotional experience would sweep through our family. The fact that my brother did not get any watches indicated that his time had run out. My niece's dad, Ray, had earlier died suddenly of a heart attack. That explained why Linda, who was not a member of our immediate family, was in the dream. Her presence would explain what was to follow. About two months after this dream, my brother Sam died suddenly of a heart attack. Both he and Ray were close to the same age, and both left this world in the same manner. I'm adding a footnote to this story. I am 85 years old as I am writing this book, and still of sound mind and body. Could the three watches that my mother gave me in a dream long ago indicate that I would be blessed with a long and healthy life?

Dreams can also predict life changing events. During the late 60's, as I started to get interested in the paranormal, I had 3 dreams that predicted a major change in my spiritual life:

A Walk in the Forest

It was nighttime. I was walking through a forest, when in the distance I saw a bright light. As I approached, I could see that it was a church. There was no door. I entered the church and found myself walking on a black marble floor. I looked around, and the walls seemed to recede. I then looked up and saw that there was no roof, and then I saw a beautiful night sky, shining with countless stars. I fell on my knees, and then a golden shaft of light fell on me.

Interpretation: This dream told me that God filled the universe and could not be contained by a building such as a church. In other words, a church should not define or limit God. The golden light told me that I should expand my feelings about the Creator, and that this would be approved by the Heavenly Realm.

Dad and I

In this dream, Dad and I went out for a ride in the family car. I did the driving. As we drove across a meadow, I suddenly saw a deep chasm in front of me. I stopped to take a look. I could not see the bottom. Dad also got out of the car. I then told him that I thought I could jump across. He immediately cautioned me not to do it. I ignored his advice, then took a running jump, and easily landed on the other side. My Dad then said that he could do it also. I yelled to him not to do it.

He ignored me, and started to run towards the chasm. He went about half way, and then to my horror, started to fall. I ran to the edge, and with a sickening thud, I heard his body hit the bottom. I stood there in total disbelief and shock. At that moment, I heard people singing. I looked down the hill below and saw that it was a small village with many people singing in the plaza. I then started happily down the hill towards the village.

Interpretation: The chasm in front of me indicated that I was to take a leap of faith in my life. My Dad represented the strict religious upbringing in my missionary family. Seeing my father jump and then fall told me that the strict religious environment I was brought up in would not project forward and thus limit my expanding view of my life journey. The singing in the village indicated the change would be a happy transformation in my life. I would like to add that I will always cherish my Christian upbringing that not only provided me with a foundation for my Christian faith, but it also gave me a strong moral base which would sustain and direct me on my life-long journey.

My sister Ruth and the dance

In this dream, I was eating out with my sister Ruth. The restaurant had a small dance floor. After listening to the unusual music the band was playing, I told Ruth that I thought I could go out on the floor and dance to the tune. She immediately said that I could not. I then got up, walked to the dance floor and easily started to dance. I asked her to join me, but she would not.

Interpretation: This dream was similar to the dream I had with my Dad. The dance and the music was a change on life's stage, but I would easily adapt to it. Ruth, again, represented my strict upbringing which I would have to move out from into a new experience.

These were my three dreams that predicted my future life. The years that followed bore this out, thus validating my dreams. Lest the reader think that I had compromised my fundamental beliefs, let me assure you that nothing could be further from the truth. My life journey would take me into a new direction that would provide me with an ever- expanding understanding of the meaning of life, and why we experience the things that confront us.

I'll close this chapter with some of the great dreams described in the Bible. The following are a few of these that come to mind:

- Genesis – Chapter 41
- In this dream, Pharaoh dreams symbols that foretold of a coming famine. Joseph, the son of Jacob, was the only one that was capable of interpreting the dreams. As predicted, the dreams came true.
- Daniel – Chapter 2
- In this dream, Nebuchadnezzar, King of Babylon, saw symbols of things to come involving future kings of Babylon. The mystery was revealed to Daniel in a dream. He was told, in the dream, details that no one knew except for Nebuchadnezzar.
- Matthew, Chapter 2
- In this dream, Joseph, the husband of Mary, mother of Jesus, was told to flee to Egypt to escape the murderous plan of King Herod to kill the baby Jesus. Everything transpired as he saw in the dream.

CHAPTER 11

THE PASSING OF MY WIFE, PHIDDY

The year was 1987. Phiddy and I owned a 34-ft travel trailer, pulled by a Suburban. We decided that year to go to Greensboro, North Carolina for a family reunion at Thanksgiving. Little did we know that a few days later, Phiddy would suffer a major heart attack and pass away. There was absolutely no forewarning of this terrible event in my life. The Thanksgiving dinner with the family, however, was one memory that I will always cherish. Early the next morning, we said our goodbye's and started our trip back to Friendswood, Texas where our home was. The trip was too long to make it in one day, so we were planning on 2 overnight stays at one of several RV parks we would encounter on our way home. The first one we found was in the northwest corner of Georgia. There, unfortunately, would occur an incident that may have played a role in the tragic event that would take place 2 days later. The Georgia campground we stayed in that first night was very large, and for the most part empty. Early the next morning, I disconnected our trailer from the camp's utilities and started to back out of our parking spot. At this time I would like to describe the size of our rig. As mentioned previously, the trailer was 34 feet long.

This was a very large trailer that had a queen-sized bedroom in the rear, a bathroom with shower, a good-sized living room with a large sofa, a nicely equipped kitchen, and finally an adjoining breakfast area. Pulling this trailer was a Chevy Suburban. The whole RV rig was a little longer than 50 ft. This is equivalent to the height of a 5-story building. To illustrate how long this was, the travel trailer had 2 small wheels in the rear so that the back-end wouldn't drag on the ground when going over a depression in the road. As I backed out, the rear started to turn on me. Lining the RV spot were large logs. The rear of the trailer went over one of these logs. We were stuck, and there was no one in sight. I got out and found part of a tree limb. Propping this under the back of the trailer, I was able to lift the rear. I was immediately faced with a problem. Phiddy didn't like to drive the rig. The limb I was using was long enough to provide good leverage. As I lifted the end of the trailer, I asked Phiddy if she could hold the limb while I got into the Suburban and drove forward enough to clear the log. Phiddy was very athletic, and she immediately said that she could do it. The whole scheme worked, and we were finally freed. We then drove during day-light hours until we reached our second RV Park. The next morning found us on our last lap home. Around noon, we had arrived at the outskirts of Vidor, Texas, a small town about 6 miles east of Beaumont, Texas.

Vidor had a long standing reputation of being all white, to the willful exclusion of African-Americans. This was particularly true during the 60's and 70's. The word around town was that African-Americans were excluded from being present in the town after dark. The Ku Klux Klan had a past history of having been very active in Vidor. Fortunately, this part of the story has a happy ending. It has been reported that African-American refugees from Hurricane Katrina's major destruction in New Orleans had been very well treated by the citizens of Vidor. The personal side of this story, unfortunately, does not end happily. Phiddy and I were getting hungry, so we stopped at one of the larger restaurants in Vidor. After finishing our meal, Phiddy went back to our trailer while I took care of the bill. When I got back to our rig, I found her sitting on the edge of the bed, breathing with large gasps. I immediately rushed back to the restaurant and yelled for an ambulance. Ten minutes later she was on the way to a hospital in Beaumont. The ambulance took off without me, and I was suddenly overwhelmed with grief. At that point, 3 men showed up. What followed made me think of these 3 men as heaven-sent "Angels". The first gentlemen said that he owned an RV park in Vidor, and would look after my trailer. The other two got into an argument as to which one would take me to Beaumont.

Finally, one of the two won out, and the next thing I knew, we were on the way to the hospital where they had taken Phiddy. During the next 2 to 3 hours, I found myself in a mental fog. I was able to get myself together sufficiently to make phone calls to the family. Around 11 P.M., the doctor came out and told me that despite all of their best efforts, Phiddy had passed away. I had a hard time taking control of my emotions. My whole world had come crashing down. This terrible happening had been so sudden. My mind was filled with memories of Phiddy and our 32-year marriage. My patient "Angel" had stood by me in the hospital, and finally took me back to my trailer. My little dog "Divot" was still in the front seat of my Suburban.

During the 70-mile trip to Friendswood, I felt that I was in another world. What followed were two small miracles. We had a parking place near Friendswood where we kept our trailer. Backing up and parking this large trailer was always a major chore, and I would usually have to make several tries. I would then, with Phiddy's help, successfully complete the maneuver. That night, however, I had help from above, and was able to park my 50-ft rig perfectly on the first try. I then proceeded tearfully to our home, where the day's second miracle took place. Phiddy had always loved to hear the honking of the flocks of Canadian geese flying to their winter nesting grounds in south Texas. The visitors from Canada always flew in a large V-formation. As I raised the garage door, I heard the familiar honking, and looked up. Silhouetted against a bright moon, I saw 2 Canadian geese fling south into the night sky. I knew then that Phiddy was still with me. This simple symbol of love and companionship provided me with a comforting feeling as I faced an empty house.

I spent that Christmas with my brother Don and his wife Iris in their home in Nokomis, Florida. The next day, after having returned to Friendswood, I received a second major shock. Paramount, the greeting card company I had worked for the last 10 years had been sold. The new owner wanted to install his own management team, so on the last day of December, 1987 I was notified that someone else would take over my job as Regional Manager, and my services were no longer needed. With this double blow, I felt that my world had come to an end. I spent the next several months crying myself to sleep. During this time, I continued pursuing my second career in sales. My sense of loss, however, persisted for several months.

In the meantime I had met someone in a new sales job I had found, who sympathized with my two losses. My new friend, who had strong religious beliefs, said that she would pray for me. I'll never forget what happened one day in June. As I mentioned earlier, I had not adjusted well to my lonely life. A miracle then happened. I awoke that morning and distinctly heard in my head the following words: "Your days of mourning are over. Behold, I make all things new!". Miraculously, from that moment on, all sense of sadness was gone. Little did I know, at that time, that later on in the year, I would meet my future wife and companion, Lovella, and, as the old saying goes: "They lived happily ever after".

CHAPTER 12

THE SECOND CALLING

It was the latter part of November, 1961. Mother and Dad were driving north on highway U.S. 1. They had just left Richmond, Virginia. Their destination was the Brazilian consulate in Baltimore, Maryland. They were planning on obtaining Visas for a trip to Brazil, South America where for the second time in their life, they wanted to open a new mission field. It was late in the day. Mother wanted to stop at the nearest motel, but Dad wanted to press on for a little while longer. This desire would soon result in a terrible accident that almost killed both of them. It was turning out to be a very cold November night. Highway U.S. 1 is a 4-lane undivided highway. As darkness fell, there was a bridge ahead that curved to the right. Unbeknown to Dad, the bridge was wet from an earlier rain. As the air temperature dropped, the surface of the bridge was turning into a sheet of ice. At the same time they reached the bridge, another car driven by a soldier was heading south and was just entering the bridge. Both cars lost complete control, and headed directly into each other. With each car going approximately 50 miles an hour, they collided head-on at a combined speed of 100 miles per hour. The only thing that prevented a 3 person fatality was that the cars hit each other slightly off center. The two cars spun around, thus absorbing some of the energy of the impact. Dad was thrown out of the car and landed on his head. A second miracle occurred. Dad survived what normally would have been a fatal blow. He was knocked unconscious and had a fracture of his lower jaw. Mother, during the spin, was thrown under the steering wheel. It took paramedics about 2 hours to free her from the wrecked car. They both were taken by ambulance to a hospital in Richmond. It was determined in the trauma unit that Mother had 36 broken bones. She later told us that the inside of her mouth felt like loose popcorn from the teeth that were knocked out of socket.

She also said that she only remembers seeing a bright light. Dad was best described as being in a twilight zone. I remember visiting him in the hospital, and he didn't even recognize me. There was a hospital orderly named Archie that would look after him. Dad told me, on one of my visits, that he planned to go to Brazil with Archie and open up a missionary field. He then went on to say: "I don't understand the Big Boss! But His Son, Him I understand". That was evidence that inside my Dad's mind there was an inner struggle to try to understand why God had let this happen to them. After all, they had worked for 40 years in the mission field in Argentina, raising a family, and overall doing good things. This brings up the old question as to why bad things happen to good people. I'll explore this universal question in my chapter on predestination and free will. Incidentally, we visited the soldier involved in the accident. Thankfully he wasn't badly injured.

Mother and Dad were in the Richmond hospital for several months. During this long stay, expenses were beginning to mount up. They both were receiving care around the clock. Some of the nurses during this period were contracted independently from outside help. I soon found myself as the go-between me and my family to cover these expenses. As time went by, I decided to visit the Christian and Missionary Alliance headquarters in New York and see if they could be of any assistance. I was told that the church did not have any resources to cover this extended hospitalization. The person I spoke to, however, told me that he would write a letter to all of the Alliance churches asking for contributions. I never told Mother and Dad what I had done. When they returned to Greensboro, a lot of money was being mailed in.

After several months in the Richmond hospital, Mother and Dad were driven back to their home in Greensboro, North Carolina. There followed several months of convalescing. During this period, I remember receiving letters from Dad. There was something unusual in these letters. Dad always signed his name in the return address on the envelope. At this time, I would like to turn back the clock to the memory of a 12-year old boy. One day, my Dad took me to downtown Buenos Aires, Argentina to one of the largest banks in the city. He had gone there to cash a check. As I watched, he carefully signed the back of the check with his familiar signature: "Samuel G. Barnes". He saw me watching him, and then said: "Son, your signature is one of the most important things you will ever possess. It attests to your honesty and commitment in life. Be sure that you always use it exactly the same way". Now, back to my parent's recovery. As mentioned earlier, there was something unusual in the letters I was receiving. Dad's signature was totally different from the one I had seen all my life. This puzzled me, until one day, months later, I got a letter from him with the old familiar signature I had always known. I knew then, that Dad was back to normal.

In September 1962, Dad decided that he had recovered sufficiently to make his long delayed trip to Brazil. When he landed in that very large country, he bought a jeep and drove out to Brasilia, the new capital of Brazil. A small historical note: Since the 19th century, the seat of government had been Rio de Janeiro. Through the years, there had always been a desire to move the capital to a more central location in the country. This goal was first defined in 1922. Finally, in 1956, the building of the new capital was started from scratch. It took 41 months to build the functioning part of the city. In April 1960, Brasilia was officially inaugurated as the capital of Brazil. Viewed from above, the main portion of the city resembles an airplane or a butterfly. When Dad visited the city in 1962, there was still construction going on. After his arrival, he met with some of the city managers, and was welcomed with open arms. The city leaders were anxious to add churches in order to enhance the stability of the new city. They offered Dad a strategically located piece of real estate to build an Alliance church. After identifying the future church site, they then said: "Reverend Barnes, we are going to add land adjacent to the church to build a parsonage". They added: "We are sure that you will want to add a second church in the future, so we are going to give you some more land in another part of the city". As Dad toured the city, he drove to the outskirts where the construction people lived. Dad describes the scene he encountered as resembling "Dodge City" from Western movies. He saw a lot of saloons, and the sound of fighting could be heard behind swinging doors. After leaving Brasilia, Dad crisscrossed Brazil, driving thousands of miles in the interior. When he left the country, he had chosen the city of Goiania as a potential future location for an Alliance church. Dad then returned to the States. In 1963, when dad was 70 years old and mother was 63, and after a horrendous car accident which they were still recovering from, my two missionary parents left for Brazil to open a new missionary field. They would spend 2 years working in this new mission field. After their return, my youngest sister Ann, and her husband Jim, would continue the missionary tradition until their retirement in 2011. A third generation would pick up the missionary banner when Ann and Jim's oldest daughter, Debbie, together with her husband Todd, would begin missionary work in Indonesia, where they continue the Lord's work to this day.

figure 12.1 [45]

BRASILIA, THE NEW CAPITAL OF BRAZIL

CHAPTER 13

THE PRESIDENTS' INTERPRETER

This is a story about my younger brother, Donald Barnes, who was the personal Spanish interpreter for 7 American presidents and one American vice president. My brother passed away on November 12, 2003. This was the same day as his first wife's, Joane, birthday. His life journey experience with so many American presidents is a story that needs to be told. He held a unique job in Washington, D.C. that transcended political parties. Although there are many individuals that have served as civil servants over many years, to my knowledge, and with the exception of the White House domestic staff, there are few if any persons who provided personal service to so many presidents, irrespective of their political affiliation. It is with a sense of great personal pride that I tell this amazing story of Don Barnes, the presidents' interpreter.

If you check the Internet, you will find the following identification of my brother: "Donald F. Barnes, interpreter in the Languages Services Division, Office of Operations, and Department of State." The real story of my brother is missing. Why? The answer lies in the position he occupied. He dealt directly and personally with the President, and what he experienced was not generally told to the journalists who followed the country's chief executive. There were times that a discussion was held between the American President and a Latin-American President, with the only other person present being my brother. With no aides at these meetings, there are no transcripts of what took place. Don was too discrete in his job to relate what transpired. I urged him to write a book about all his experiences with so many presidents, but sadly, he never seemed to find the time, or the energy to do this. It is up to me, therefore, to tell some of his amazing experiences. I should state at the outset, that I will describe only personal anecdotes, and not any state matters. After all, isn't this what is missing from presidential stories?

The Beginning of His Career.

Don was born in the city of Azul, Argentina, as I was. The whole family of eight was bi-lingual. It should be pointed out that aside from the missionary work, no one in the family, except for Don, would use the Spanish language in their professional life. I believe that professional interpreters are born with a language skill. Don once told me there were only about 300 what he called true professional first class interpreters in the country. This was across all languages. What a small select group in a country of more than 300 million. At this time, I would like to differentiate between a translator and an interpreter. The translator deals with translating documents and other examples of the written word, whereas the interpreter is faced with translating the spoken word in real time. There are two types of interpreting: One is called "simultaneous interpreting" and the other is called "consecutive interpreting". Both present unusual challenges to the interpreter. During simultaneous interpreting, it is necessary for the interpreter to follow the speaker almost word for word. My brother once told me that his mind picks up on a key word being spoken, and then anticipates how the sentence will be completed. During all this, he must quickly come up with an American colloquial expression matching the one being used by the Latin-American guest. Add to this, that the voice inflection should match the voice of the foreign dignitary, and vice versa. All of this is to be accomplished many times at a fast pace. My brother would tell me there would occur somewhat of a union between his mind and the president's mind. He described this as a natural rhythm. Rapid speech did not seem to be a problem. Consecutive interpreting presented a different challenge. He would listen for two or so minutes to what the president was saying, and then he would reconstruct the speech lines with the same tone and inflection as that spoken by the president. This meant being forceful, angry, consoling, descriptive, etc., etc. Now you see why I believe that outstanding interpreters are born with a special gift. The fact that Don was called on by seven American presidents to travel with them in Air Force One attests to his skills.

Now back to my story. The date was June 25, 1950. My wife Phiddy and I were visiting Don and his wife Joane in Washington, D.C. We were driving around in Don's convertible when, all of a sudden, the music we were listening to stopped, and we heard the attention getting words: "We are interrupting this program to bring you an important bulletin". To this day, when these words are spoken, one feels their stomach turning while you wait for the bulletin, which you know, will always be bad news. The announcer, in a few words, said that North Korean troops had invaded South Korea. Little did I dream that my older brother Sam would soon be shipped to the Korean Peninsula, with only 48-hours' notice to say good bye to his family. The four of us looked at each other with great surprise, knowing that in all probability the United States would ultimately be involved in a new Pacific war.

Later on that day, we discussed the beginning of Don's career as an interpreter. He was 20 years old at that time, and had just started work in the State Department as a clerk/typist. He began to accumulate experience translating documents into Spanish. One year later, an opportunity presented itself to work with The Organization of American States, known as the OAS. This provided him with very useful experience in interpreting.

THE JAPANESE PEACE CONFERENCE.

The year was 1951. A major international event took place in San Francisco. Fifty one nations met in that city, and on September 8, 1951, forty eight of the attending nations signed a peace treaty with Japan, thus ending World War II. Three nations, (Czechoslovakia, Poland, and the Soviet Union), refused to sign the document. The head of the Soviet Union delegation was Soviet Foreign Minister Andrei Gromyko, and there-in lies a story that was witnessed by my brother. At the time, Don was 21 years old. A large delegation of interpreters from the State Department, headed by their supervisor who happened to be the one who handled the Russian language, were located in a booth removed from the main assembly room. In those days, television was still undergoing growing pains, so broadcast radio was still counted on to inform the American public. Don, being the junior man on the interpreting team, was given the job of interpreting governor of California Earl Warren's welcoming speech to the international peace treaty conference. (A historical note: This is the same Earl Warren who would go on to become Chief Justice of the United States Supreme Court. In that fateful year of 1963, when we lost our president, Jack Kennedy, to an assassin's bullet, Justice Warren was appointed by President Johnson to head up an investigative group charged with unearthing the real story behind JFK's assassination. (This select group would forever be remembered as "The Warren Commission"). The Japanese Peace Conference was a very exciting event in my brother's life. Another unplanned event, however, occurred which almost resulted in an international uproar. As stated earlier, our interpreters were located in a booth near the conference room. In this booth was a microphone which controlled access to the nation's radio network. On the mike was a switch. In the "On" position, the national radio network was "live". In the other position it was disconnected. The Soviet Minister, Andrei Gromyko, had made a very long speech outlining the Soviet Union's objection to the treaty. Our American interpreter handling this long harangue was taxed to the limit. Finally, Mr. Gromyko ended his very long speech. Our exhausted interpreter reached for the microphone and thought that he had turned it off. Unfortunately, he had not, and the mike was still live coast-to-coast. Totally worn out, he yelled: "That Russian S.O.B." (He actually spelled out the three words). When Gromyko heard of this, he immediately demanded an apology, and a punishment of our poor interpreter.

figure 13.1 [46]

CHIEF JUSTICE EARL WARREN 10/53 – 6/69

CALIFORNIA GOVERNOR 1/43 – 10/53

figure 13.2 [47]

ANDREI GROMYKO

RUSSIA'S FOREIGN MINISTER

It should be noted that at this time the "Cold War" between the United States and the Soviet Union was well underway. Needless to say, neither demand was met!

In the meantime, Don had begun to attend George Washington University in Washington, D.C. Later on he graduated with a degree in international studies.

THE PRESIDENT DWIGHT D. EISENHOWER YEARS

When President Eisenhower was elected president by a landslide in 1952, he brought with him Vernon Walters as a staff member. Walters, according to my brother Don, was a first rate interpreter fluent in French, Italian, Spanish, Portuguese, and German. He served as an aide and interpreter for several Presidents. He went on to have a very long and distinguished career serving his country in many ways, and through various assignments. His knowledge of Spanish and his long familiarity with Eisenhower meant that Walters would have a favored position as interpreter for Ike. Nevertheless, there were some high moments in Don's career during the Eisenhower years. He first interpreted for President Eisenhower in 1957, during visits by the presidents of Guatemala and Costa Rica.

The following is one of the major events in Don's professional life:

ADDRESS TO A JOINT SESSION OF CONGRESS.

The story unfolds on January 21, 1959. The recently elected president of Argentina, Arturu Frondizi, having received a formal invitation from President Eisenhower, paid a state visit to the United States.

My brother Don, would play a significant role in the success of Frondizi's visit. Evidence of this would come sometime later in far away Argentina. In re-telling this experience, Don said that when you are standing in the House of Representatives chamber, you see before you: (1) All of the Supreme Court justices; (2) The top military commanders of our armed forces; (3) The President's Cabinet; (4) Ambassadors from all of the Latin American countries; (5) All members of the U.S. Senate; and finally (6) All members of the U.S. House of Representatives. He said that this is an overwhelming emotional experience. On top of it all, is the realization that his interpreting would go a long way in determining the success of President Frondizi's visit. One other incident occurred before the address to Congress, and attests to the professional capabilities of Don. The date was January 21, 1959, the day before the congressional speech. A meeting which was attended by Don took place between the U.S. ambassador to Argentina and Mr. Frondizi. According to records in the State Department central files, "the Argentine president was presented with two memorandums of the meeting, one by the U.S. ambassador to Argentina, and one by Donald Barnes". In a highly unusual incident, Mr. Frondizi asked for a copy of Don's memorandum for his personal use. Rarely, if ever, is the interpreter's name mentioned in the formal documents of these meetings. In an internal State Department memo dated March 4, 1959, a staff member states that Barnes' version provided greater details than the official version drafted by the U.S. Ambassador. The memo goes on to state that the two versions agreed with each other.

The story picks up now in Argentina, sometime later. My Mother was living in Buenos Aires. One morning there is a knock on the door. When she opened it, there stood a distinguished looking lady, and at the curb was a long black limousine. The visitor then said "I am Mrs. Frondizi, the president's wife, and I want to personally thank you for the outstanding services of your son, Don Barnes, during my husband's recent visit to the United States. Don played a major role in the success of my husband's visit". At the beginning of this story, I stated that evidence of Don's professionalism would occur sometime after Frondizi's visit. Now the reader knows the basis for this statement.

figure 13.3 [48]

ARGENTINE PRESIDENT FRONDIZI & FAMILY

figure 13.4 [49]

DON BARNES WITH PRESIDENT EISENHOWER

(He is the second from the left)

THE PRESIDENT JOHN F. KENNEDY YEARS

On January 20, 1961, the newly elected John F. Kennedy gave his famous inaugural address. This speech is listed by most historians among the top four inaugural addresses of all the U.S. Presidents. The Voice Of America, VOA, is the official international broadcast institution of the United States Federal Government. On January 20, 1961, my brother Don was honored with the assignment to interpret into Spanish, in real time, President Kennedy's inaugural address. His interpretation reached millions of people in Latin America.

Trip to Venezuela & Columbia

An interesting incident occurred during a trip JFK made to visit President Betancourt, the Venezuelan president. My brother was flying with JFK aboard Air Force One. While they were crossing over the Caribbean Sea, Kennedy asked his aide, who was a brigadier general, to go to the cockpit and ask the pilot to find out what the weather would be like in Caracas, (the Venezuelan capital). Kennedy was scheduled to make a speech in an open air stadium that afternoon. The general went to the cockpit and engaged the pilot in long conversations about old war stories. After some time, the general exclaimed: "I almost forgot to ask you to contact the tower at Caracas and find out what the weather would be like in the early afternoon". The pilot said that, at that time of year, it would be mild and sunny. The aide went back and gave JFK his weather report. Kennedy was wearing a dark suit, and upon hearing the weather forecast, decided not to change into lighter clothes. That afternoon, Kennedy found himself melting in a temperature ten degrees hotter than what he had been told. During his interpreting, my brother felt a jab in his back and heard "Speak up Don! Put more enthusiasm in your voice". My brother responded by raising his voice and moving his arms as he spoke. The response from the crowd was immediate as they roared back with every phrase. Don told me afterwards that he now understands why political leaders get intoxicated by the response of crowds during their speeches.

The president later on flew to Bogota, the capital of Columbia. During a formal speech he gave earlier in the day, another incident involving my brother took place. Kennedy had given Don an advanced copy of the speech he was to give that day. Don noticed an error had been made on a historical fact. He corrected it before the speech was made. Later, Kennedy, with a very serious face, said, "I understand that you corrected my speech". Don answered "Yes, Mr. President". Kennedy then smiled and said "Thank you very much". That evening, both he and his lady, Jackie, were invited to a sumptuous banquet. Following a few after-dinner words by Kennedy, he turned around to Jackie and said "I would now like to introduce someone who doesn't need an interpreter". My brother, being the consummate interpreter that he was, moved the President aside to get to the microphone to translate Kennedy's few words. This took Kennedy somewhat aback, but then he turned around and smiled at Don. On the way back to the States in Air Force One, there occurred an incident rarely witnessed. The President was sitting at a table talking about the previous day's events, when he suddenly stopped and said "Get me my aide". Don then witnessed the President of the United States chewing out a brigadier general. Kennedy, using very salty language from his Navy days, dressed down his aide for not properly reporting the hot weather during the Venezuelan speech. The poor general could only stand there and say "I'm sorry sir, it won't happen again". After about a minute, Kennedy suddenly said "Dismissed!" There are two footnotes to this story. The first was that nothing more was ever said by the President on this incident, and nothing ever appeared on the general's record. The second note adds a little spice to the story. It was found out later that the First Lady, previously known as Jacqueline Bouvier, had dated the general before she was married and JFK knew it.

Trip to Mexico

It should be noted, that at the outset, Kennedy had developed a mistrust of interpreters because of mistakes by an interpreter during a trip he had made to Paris. This was to change dramatically, when after a very successful trip to Mexico, Don received a letter of commendation from Kennedy for the outstanding job he had done during the Mexican visit. The trip to Mexico took place in July, 1962. Kennedy and Jackie had been invited by the Mexican president, Lopez Mateos, to visit Mexico City. During their visit, they stayed at the new luxury Maria Isabel Hotel in downtown Mexico City. During a banquet that evening, a well-publicized incident took place. Jackie Kennedy had been listening to Lopez Mateos. When he finished speaking, she complemented him on his strong and deep speaking voice. Mateos, well known as a "Ladies Man", thought that Jackie was "coming on" to him. He then pulled out a beautiful cigarette lighter. At that moment Jackie exclaimed "What a beautiful lighter!" The tradition in Mexico is that means "I want the lighter". The press later reported that she kept the lighter. Then, in a later conversation, President Mateos told Kennedy "You have a beautiful wife!" At that time, it was reported that JFK said "Give him back the lighter, Jackie!"

During JFK's administration, he became concerned over political instability in Central America. He set up a committee chaired by General Alexander Hague to oversee developments in this vital area. JFK made his first trip to this region by visiting Costa Rica, a model of democracy. Costa Rica was famous for having a lot of pretty women. As they drove through the capital of San Jose, JFK said "What am I doing driving down in a motorcade when my staff are having fun with the pretty Costa Rican women?" Don, who was sitting with the President in the limousine, looked at him thinking that he was kidding. To his surprise, by the expression on JFK's face, he realized that he wasn't kidding.

figure 13.5 [50]

JACK KENNEDY VISITING IN COSTA RICA

(DON IS TO HIS LEFT)

figure 13.6 [51]

PRESIDENT JACK KENNEDY

figure 13.7 [52]

JACKIE KENNEDY

figure 13.8 [53]

MEXICAN PRESIDENT LOPEZ MATEOS

THE BAY OF PIGS INVASION

A little known fact about the Bay of Pigs invasion was that planning started under the Eisenhower administration. In March of 1960, President Eisenhower approved a document by the National Security Council to prepare a plan that would ultimately remove Fidel Castro as the Cuban leader. In April 1960, the CIA started recruiting anti-Castro Cuban exiles in the Miami area. Their objective was to prepare a Cuban exile brigade that would ultimately invade Cuba and overthrow Castro's regime. The plan originally was to invade Cuba near a town by the name of Trinidad. The town had both good port facilities and a defensible beachhead. When Jack Kennedy started his administration in January, 1961, the State Department undertook an examination of the Trinidad Plan, and concluded that it had too much visibility and might compromise the United States. It was then that an alternative plan called "The Bay of Pigs Plan" was adopted. This story has a sad ending. The invasion lasted from April 17, 1961 to April 20, 1961, and ended with a total defeat of the Cuban exiles brigade. Kennedy did not wish to start a full-out war with Cuba, and did not provide direct air support. The surviving Cuban exile members were picked up by U.S. Navy ships and brought back to American soil. The brigade soldiers captured by the Cubans were later ransomed by the United States. On December 29, 1962, President Kennedy attended a "Welcome Back" ceremony for the Cuban exiles brigade. It was held at the Orange Bowl in Miami.

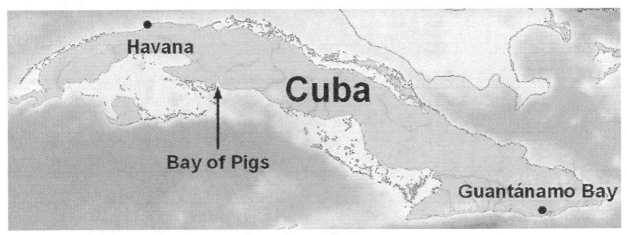

figure 13.9 [54]

BAY OF PIGS

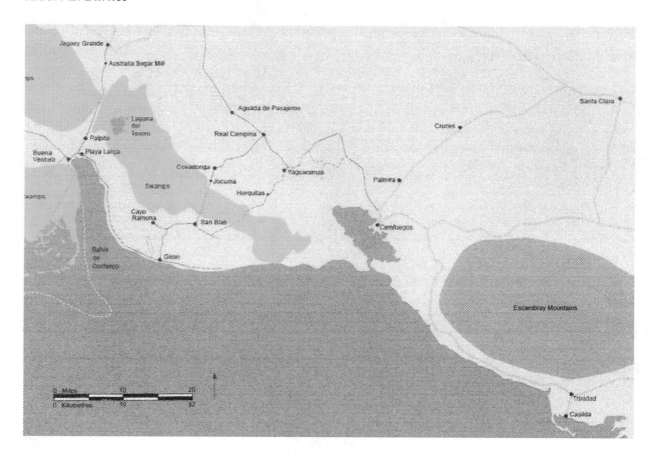

figure 13.10 [55]

BAY OF PIGS

SPANISH: (" BAHIA DE COCHINOS")

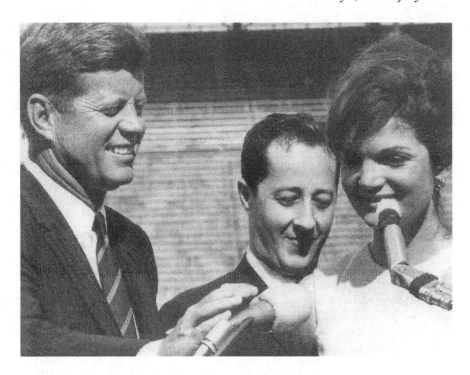

figure 13.11 [56]

JACK & JACKIE KENNEDY @ THE ORANGE BOWL

(IN THE CENTER, DON BARNES)

The Miami Cubans planned to boycott the ceremony, bitter over what they considered to be Kennedy's betrayal of the invasion by withholding U.S. air support. Rumors of an alleged bomb at the stadium, however, caused them to rally, and Kennedy won them over with a rousing and militant speech. Incidentally, the speech omitted entire paragraphs in the prepared text which addressed the need for democracy and social reform in Latin America. Don told me later that he felt as if he was in the center of a "bull's eye".

A very humorous event took place with Don's young son, Craig. It was early evening, and suddenly the phone rang in Don's home. Young Mr. Craig was near the phone and answered it. He heard a man's voice ask "Is Don Barnes there"? Craig immediately asked "Who is calling"? The voice said "The president". Craig then asked "The president of what"? Don told us later that JFK got a big charge out of the call. This is a good time to illustrate the difference between Kennedy's predecessor, President Eisenhower, and JFK. Eisenhower, being a military man, always used the chain of command. In this particular type of situation, for example, if he wanted a Spanish interpreter, he would ask an aide to call the State Department, the person in the State Department answering the call would, in most cases, alert the Secretary of State that the President was asking for an interpreter. This would be followed by an office aide being instructed to call my brother Don. The contrast with Kennedy is obvious. JFK's relationship with Don was "one-on-one".

The Death of a President

Late in November, 1963, President Kennedy planned a fund-raising trip to Dallas, Texas. Several people, including our U.N. Ambassador Adlai Stevenson, warned JFK against coming to Dallas, but Kennedy refused their advice. A few days before the trip, Kennedy called my brother Don. He told him that he was planning a trip to Texas with Jackie. Jackie was planning to accompany him on a side trip to San Antonio where he would be giving a dedication speech for the U.S. Air Force School of Aerospace Medicine at Brooks Air Force Base.

The first leg of the journey took JFK and Jackie to Houston, Texas. There his plane had landed at Ellington Air Force Base, a small air field near NASA's Manned Spacecraft Center, later to be renamed "The Johnson Space Center". A little incident involving "yours truly" occurred during JFK's motorcade trip to Houston. At that time, I was working at G.E.'s NASA Support Center a few miles south of Houston. Word got around that Kennedy's car would be passing by our office that afternoon on the way to Houston. The small group I was in was lined up near the highway being used by Kennedy's motorcade. As his limousine passed by, one of my G.E. friends exclaimed how easy it would be to take a shot at him. My brother was riding in a bus with the press corp. about 20 cars back of the President's limousine. He told me later that as the bus passed the G.E. group, he said to a reporter sitting next to him, "I think I see someone that looks like my brother". Later on, the next afternoon, while I was working in my office, my friend suddenly appeared in the doorway with a very strange look on his face. He said "Al, my comment about President Kennedy just came true"!

Back to the first day: When the motorcade arrived in Houston, Kennedy said that Jackie was to give a speech that evening at a dinner sponsored by The League of United Latin American citizens, (LULAC). She had wanted my brother Don to accompany them on the trip to Texas to translate her speech. Later on, Don would say "Jackie's accent was good, but her Spanish was not". After the dinner, JFK invited Don to go on to Dallas with them. The following day, November 22, 1963, would go down in history as the day our president had been assassinated. Don was in the press bus that fateful day, several cars back. They heard some kind of commotion up front, but had no idea as to what had happened. The first indication of something wrong, was the rush of police cars roaring by. Don would return to Washington in Air Force 2. Four days later, in an edition dated November 23, 1963,The San Juan Star, out of San Juan, Puerto Rico, published a noteworthy article on Don's reaction to President Kennedy's death.

THE SAN JUAN STAR — Tuesday, November 26, 1963. 31

HE DRAFTED SPEECH FOR MRS. KENNEDY

J.F.K.'s Interpreter Stunned

By BEN F. MEYER

WASHINGTON — Donald Barnes, widely known to U. S. television audiences as the third, unidentified man in conferences of President John F. Kennedy with Latin American leaders, is proficient in Spanish and English, but Saturday he found it hard to express himself.

Barnes is a State Department interpreter and accompanied President Kennedy on trips to Venezuela, Colombia, Mexico, Costa Rica, Miami, and also attended many White House conferences.

On the wall just above Barnes's desk is a letter from President Kennedy praising his work, and in the late President's own hand writing:

"You did a first class job."

It referred to Barnes's services on the Mexican trip, when Mexicans by the thousands turned out for President and Mrs. Kennedy on a good will trip and also for the speeches which Barnes interpreted.

Barnes sat at his desk in the State Department Saturday and said the President's assassination "still seems untrue; it is sort of like a nightmare."

A reporter commented on the President's letter on the wall and Barnes choked up and said:

"It was one of the many heart-warming things he did."

Barnes accompanied the Kennedy's on their trip to Texas this week.

"The President telephoned me at my home Wednesday night and said: 'I wonder if you would be good enough to help Mrs. Kennedy out on a speech she wants to make.'

I thought he meant going down to the White House, and I of course said I would be pleased. Then he told me the plane would leave the following morning and asked me to be on board."

The interpreter said Mrs. Kennedy "has a very good pronunciation in Spanish, as she also speaks French and Italian, but she had to be sure the talk she was making to Texans of Mexican origin in Houston was in good order. We drafted it on the plane."

Barnes said President Kennedy normally talked at a pace giving him time for good enunciation and the listeners an opportunity to hear what he said. "But sometimes, on press conferences, for example, some of the reporters sometimes clocked him in short bursts at 400 words a minute.

"On the Latin American speeches he developed a rhythm and when he paused I would come in with a translation.

"He seemed to have a very deep interest in Latin America, and indicated various times he was much impressed by their vigor. The President seemed also to have a wonderful feel for people. You could almost see the crowd going along with him as he spoke."

Barnes was born in Buenos Aires, Argentina, __ years ago, of U. S. parents who were missionaries. They are now in Guiana, an outpost in Brazil. He lived in Argentina until 17, and learned Spanish and English both as he grew up.

figure 13.12 [57]

ARTICLE IN THE SAN JUAN STAR

(PUBLISHED IN SAN JUAN, PUERTO RICO)

GOODBYE IN MEXICO (JULY, 1962)

President Kennedy breaks into a big smile as Mexican girl eludes security guards and runs to him for a farewell hug at Mexico City's airport, just before the President and Mrs. Kennedy left for home. The girl then got a hug from Mrs. Kennedy.

figure 13.13 [58]

(Don Barnes is in the middle, just back of the Kennedy's)

(AP Wirephoto, Syracuse Herald-Journal, 7-2-62)

PRESIDENT LYNDON JOHNSON YEARS

After the assassination of President Kennedy, my brother Don underwent a major re-adjustment in his relationship with the presidency. LBJ's personality was totally different from JFK's. As a result of Don's professionalism, however, Don would later say that LBJ became fond of him, a strange accolade to describe a president-to-interpreter relationship. An early incident occurred during a trip LBJ made to El Salvador in Central America. Don was riding with the press behind Johnson. The Secret Service told him that he wasn't needed in the president's car. Suddenly he heard that LBJ was going to stop to shake hands with the crowds that lined up to see him. The Secret Service immediately tells Don to catch up with the President's limousine. When he got into the car, LBJ sat there glaring at him. Then later he is heard to say: "Does that Barnes think he's here on a (blankety blank) vacation". After a banquet that evening, LBJ, sitting in the back of his limo, said: "When Don Barnes realizes that he and I are a team, we work pretty well together". From that moment on, Johnson began to trust Don.

During the early part of his tenure as president LBJ invited the president of Mexico, Diaz Ordaz, to visit him at his ranch near Johnson City, Texas. Greeting the Mexican President, were both President Johnson and his wife Lady Bird. My brother was on hand to provide the necessary interpreting. Don would later say that he found the ranch to be comfortable but rustic. Later, he made the comment that he found Lady Bird to be a marvelous First Lady, and, he added, very intelligent. He re-counted that during the planning of a visit to Mexico, Lady Bird sent her press secretary, Liz Carpenter, to Don and told him that she wanted to make a speech in Spanish during her upcoming visit. Don told Liz: "The Texas drawl is delightful, but it makes a mess out of the Spanish language".

In October 1967, President Johnson met with the Mexican president, Diaz Ordaz, on the Mexican border, and formally proclaimed the settlement of what was known as the "Chamizal Dispute". This boundary dispute between the United States and Mexico resulted from natural shifts in the Rio Grande River.

Another trip abroad also took place in 1967. President Johnson and Secretary of State Dean Rusk traveled to the resort town of "Punta del Este" in Uruguay. The meeting was held with the heads of state of Latin American countries Common Market. (See photo).

figure 13.14 [59]

PRESIDENT JOHNSON WITH THE PRESIDENT OF URUGUAY

(Don Barnes is in the Middle)

Toward the end of President Johnson's administration, Don flew to Mexico with Vice President Hubert Humphrey to represent the U.S. at the signing of a Latin-American treaty establishing a Latin-American Nuclear-Free Zone. Don stayed in the hotel with Humphrey, while Johnson addressed the nation. He was listening to Johnson on a short-wave radio, and interpreting for President Diaz Ordaz what the American president was saying. Don felt there was something in the air when he heard LBJ say: "I've decided ---------------," and at that moment, Don's interpreter's mind anticipated him saying "not to campaign actively". Instead, Johnson completed the statement: "not to run for re-election". At that moment, Hubert Humphrey became the next Democratic candidate for president of the United States!

One final anecdote in LBJ's life: In the basement of the White House is a very large shop, outfitted to make electrical, plumbing, painting, etc. repairs. There was a master switch that controlled the lights in the shop. At that time, LBJ was on a campaign to conserve electricity in the White House. A repairman was working in the shop, one night, when he heard footsteps, and then saw a hand reach out and kill all of the shop lights. The repairman finds the switch and turns on the lights again. This happened two or three times. The workman then yells: "Will that stupid idiot who keeps turning off my lights let me do my work!" He then hears footsteps walking away. The next day, a memo was issued by the Oval Office to have each work area's lighting to be controlled by its own switch.

A closing note: Don tells me that Dean Rusk, the Secretary of State who served for 8 years under President Kennedy and President Johnson had a troubled career. Rusk believed that his primary job was to serve the President. In this capacity, he did not always provide the independent voice necessary to contribute to policy making decisions. One other factor that over the years influenced the protracted Vietnam War was his belief in the "Domino Theory". According to this theory, Communism would spread from country to country until the whole region would end up under Communist control. This, of course, was true with Hitler during World War II. The validity of this theory was applied in Southeast Asia and was a major factor in leading to the expansion of the Vietnam War. The "Domino Theory" may have been true at the time, but only history will be the final arbiter.

PRESIDENT RICHARD M. NIXON YEARS

President Nixon once introduced my brother Don with these words: "This is Mr. Barnes, whose English is better than his Spanish, and whose Spanish is better than his English". Don later said that Nixon enjoyed hearing his words in Spanish.

Trip to Puerto Vallarta, Mexico

In August 1970, Don made his only foreign travel with President Nixon, to Puerto Vallarta, Mexico. There he would meet with the Mexican President, Diaz Ordaz. Accompanying Nixon was Henry Kissenger, who was his National Security Advisor, later to become his Secretary of State. Kissenger had a phobia about using American interpreters. He would rather use foreign interpreters. Don's comment on this idiosyncrasy was that a psychiatrist would have to analyze that problem. When Kissenger asked the Mexican President who was going to be his interpreter, Diaz Ordaz was heard to say that he thought that something would be very wrong between

Mexican and American relations if Mr. Barnes was not present. Later, the Mexican President said that Mr. Barnes was a major factor in the relationship between Mexico and the United States. This was an astonishing statement, to say the least, and was intended, I'm sure, to express a compliment about Don's outstanding interpreting work. At the conclusion of the meeting, Diaz Ordaz said that his interpreters had prettier legs than the American interpreter. Don started to say that he hadn't seen his, but thought better of it.

Second Address to a Joint Session of Congress

On June 15, 1972, Don participated in his second address to a joint session of congress. The occasion was a state visit by Luis Echeverria, the President of Mexico.

figure 13.15 [60]

PRESIDENT NIXON (left) WITH LUIS ECHEVERRIA

(REVIEWING U.S. TROOPS (1972)

Don had several interpreting sessions at the Nixon White House. He went on to say that he never felt comfortable around the President. He did say that he thought that Nixon was a brilliant man, but that he had a dark side to him. Nixon once related that he had never got a teddy bear from his Mother when he was a child. He considered this to be a blight on his childhood, implying that his Mother was very undemonstrative. After Nixon's resignation in August, 1974, he was succeeded by the Vice President, Gerald Ford. Don interpreted for President Ford only once or twice, and considered him to be a little on the dull side.

figure 13.16 [61]

RICHARD M. NIXON

37TH U. S. President

figure 13.17 [62]

GERALD FORD

38TH U.S. President

figure 13.18 [63]

PRESIDENT NIXON AND PRESIDENT ECHEVERRIA

(Don Barnes on Far Right)

PRESIDENT JIMMY CARTER YEARS

During Jimmy Carter's presidency, Don primarily attended to his administrative duties as Chief of the State Department's Interpreting Branch. Don made a comment that President Carter liked to think that he spoke Spanish, but actually not very much. His most important involvement with Latin America was in negotiating the 1977 Torrijos-Carter Treaties that eventually gave Panama full sovereignty over the Panama Canal. One personal comment from my brother about President Carter: "His facial expressions, particularly his eyes, were very cold".

figure 13.19 [64]

JIMMY CARTER

39TH U.S. President

figure 13.20 [65]

Jimmy Carter and Omar Torrijos

(Signing of Panama Canal Treaty, 9/77)

figure 13.21 [66]

PRESIDENT CARTER WITH LATIN AMERICAN PRESIDENT

(DON BARNES STANDING)

The President Reagan Years

One of the most significant events my brother Don participated in during Reagan's tenure as president came to be known as "The Falklands War". The two countries involved were Argentina and Great Britain. The history of this conflict goes back many years. Argentina's claims for these barren islands started in the 1800's, even though Great Britain ruled over the Falklands for most of the time, up to the present.

The year is 1982. Tension between Argentina and the United Kingdom (U.K.) began to grow early in the year, and fear of open hostilities was developing in the U.S. President Reagan then ordered General Alexander Haig, his Secretary of State, to try and see if he could forestall an armed conflict between Argentina and the U.K.

The plan was for Haig to commute between London and Buenos Aires, working diplomatic exchanges between the two countries. In April 1982, Haig started what was known as "Shuttle Diplomacy". For a time, he thought that he was making good progress. Unfortunately, the Argentine general who was the acting president was drunk most of the time, so Haig was left to deal with second-tier Argentine administration officials. My brother, Don, was in on the negotiations, but Haig met with a serious logistical problem. At that time, Argentina was ruled by a Junta of three military chiefs, one each for the Army, Navy, and Air Force. A "no!" from any of the three killed the agreement. During this whole discussion, Haig shuttled back and forth from London to Buenos Aires, while Don anchored things in Argentina. Don was told by a counter-part in the Argentine Foreign Ministry: "Great Britain has one parliament, while we have three". During these negotiations, Don worked from 11 A.M. one day to 2 A.M. the next day. At one time, Haig thought that he had succeeded in preventing hostilities between the two countries. He did, however, tell the Argentine negotiating officials, that after one round is fired, the U.S. would no longer be neutral. Unfortunately, the Argentine general who was the acting president from the Junta decided that it was time to retake the Falkland Islands (called Islas Malvinas by the Argentines) from the British. He would go to a large map and say that there was no way, because of the distances, that the British would defend the islands. Also, they didn't believe that a woman prime minister (Margaret Thatcher) would have the nerve to intervene. (They didn't know the "Iron Lady").

American satellites provided information on the Argentine preparations for the invasion. Reagan called the Argentine president and told him that it would be a big mistake to invade the islands. After the war was underway, Margaret Thatcher committed, what some thought, a cold, and bloody act. There was an old battleship that at one time belonged to the U.S. The ship originally was the U.S. Phoenix. It was sold to Argentina where it was re-named the "Manuel Belgrano". The battleship had over 1000 cadets and sailors aboard and was reported to be steaming away from the battlefield, when it was sunk by the British nuclear-powered submarine "HMS Conqueror" on May 2, 1982. Approximately 323 members, mostly young naval cadets, died in the incident. Over 700 men were rescued from the ocean despite cold seas and stormy weather. The losses from the "Belgrano" totaled nearly half of the Argentine deaths in the conflict. Finally, after nearly three months, hostilities between the two countries ended, after the British had successfully defended the islands. Total casualties from both sides were 907 killed and 1843 wounded. Don stated that the sinking of the battleship "Belgrano" probably saved Margaret Thatcher's election, because prior to this incident, it had been reported that she was losing. She went on to establish a record as Prime Minister, having served for over 11 years. The war ended on June 14, 1982 with the British retaining control over the Falkland Islands. The loss of the Falkland Islands War by Argentina discredited the military and basically removed them from political power.

figure 13.22 [67]

GENERAL ALEXANDER HAIG

figure 13.23 [68]

PRIME MINISTER MARGARET THATCHER

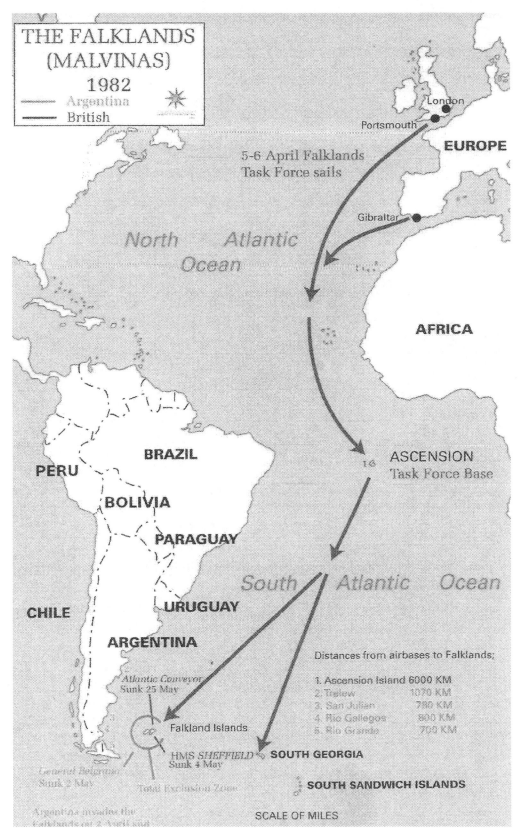

figure 13.24 [69]

THE ARGENTINE-BRITISH FALKLAND ISLANDS WAR

figure 13.25 [70]

THE ARGENTINE BATTLESHIP

"GENERAL BELGRANO"

Meetings With Foreign Visitors

On one occasion, Reagan was taking the visiting Dominican President on a mini-tour of the White House offices. They came to the Roosevelt Room, where Reagan showed a plaque on the wall commemorating President Teddy Roosevelt receiving a Nobel Prize. The Dominican President then asked when was Teddy Roosevelt president. Reagan then answered "I have no idea"! My brother Don, who was nearby to interpret the conversations, quickly answered "In the early part of the century".

During formal bi-lateral meetings with foreign dignitaries, Reagan always had his 3x5 cards from which he would read his prepared statements. He would sit silent, with no writing pads or extemporaneous notes in front of him. He would, however, respond to the discussions with smiles and nods of his head.

Trip To Spain

In March 1985 President Reagan went to Europe on a less than successful trip, what with an unfortunate visit to a Nazi cemetery in West Germany and a cool reception in Madrid. Prior to departure from that city, there was an informal meeting in the airport VIP lounge. This was Don's last trip abroad with President Reagan. In discussing this trip, Don goes back to his first interpreting assignment with Reagan. He was told that the President was hard of hearing in one ear. During his interpreting, Don spoke loudly in Regan's left ear. When he saw the President jump, he realized that he was yelling into the wrong ear. During the trip to Spain, Don was riding in the 6th car behind the President. Suddenly, the presidential limousine stopped. The Secret Service told Don to get out and run to the President's limousine in case he was needed for interpreting. Don immediately answered that, for his own personal safety, under no condition would he run to the President's car.

Final Comments On The Reagan Presidency.

Don said that President Reagan, above all, loved his country. He was always friendly, polite, and gracious in dealing with everybody around him. He was also, according to Don, the best story teller that he had ever run across. Finally, he took a sincere interest in the world around him, and could inspire all of those he encountered, with his contagious optimism.

figure 13.26 [71]

RONALD REAGAN

40th PRESIDENT OF THE UNITED STATES

figure 13.27 [72]

**KING JUAN CARLOS, PRESIDENT REAGAN,
DONALD BARNES**

(From left)

VICE PRESIDENT GEORGE H. W. BUSH

On January 20, 1981, George H. W. Bush, the father of the future President George W. Bush, was inaugurated as the 43rd Vice President of the United States. Even though Bush understood some Spanish, Don interpreted for him on several occasions. My brother developed a good relationship with both Vice President Bush and his wife, Barbara. Don went on to say that Bush and his wife liked him and vice versa. He said that Bush was fun to travel with, and took a very good "crew" with him. There was a lot of joke telling and laughter during these trips. When Don retired from his interpreting job, Bush sent him a very nice autographed photo with words of appreciation for a job well done. (Note: See who was sitting behind the desk in the photo).

One final word on Don's 30-year career as the presidents' interpreter: His biography was given to each new incoming U.S. President. Don never saw it. His "Top Secret" security clearance was always updated periodically.

I lost my wonderful brother (another missionary's son) to cancer on November 12, 2003, and I will miss him forever!

figure 13.28 [73]

GEORGE H.W. BUSH

U.S. Vice President - Jan. 20, 1989 to Jan.20, 1993

figure 13.29 [74]

PRESIDENT OF ECUADOR, (Left), DON BARNES, VICE PRESIDENT BUSH

figure 13.30 [75]

AL AND DON BARNES

TWO MISSIONARY'S SONS; TWO BROTHERS; TWO FRIENDS

CHAPTER 14

THE HAUNTED HOUSE

This is the story of a house Lovella and I had rented in Biloxi, Mississippi. The year was 1999 and we had just moved from Mobile, Alabama. The house, located on Bayview Ave. in east Biloxi, faced Back Bay, which was approximately one mile north of the Gulf of Mexico. Back Bay was connected directly to the Gulf. All my life I have wanted to live near water. When we moved to Biloxi, my dream finally came true, and I had a beautiful 1-mile view across Back Bay. To our immediate left lived our landlady, Tanya Gollott, in a 2-story Victorian house. Tanya's dad was Tommy Gollott, a name very famous in this part of Mississippi. Tommy was a Mississippi senator, and was one of the major influences, (through his efforts in the Mississippi legislature), in bringing casino gambling to the Mississippi Gulf coast. The house the Gollott's were living in was a small one-story building around the corner from us. They had raised three daughters, including Tanya. The relationships between the Gollott family and Lovella and I would, over the next 5 to 6 years, evolve to the point that we felt like we were treated as members of the family. Between Tanya's house and the Gollott's older home, Tommy was building a multi-story house with large white columns both in front and in back. The overall structure looked like a governor's mansion. The house we rented originally belonged to Tommy's parents.

His Dad's name was Houston. We were told by Tommy that his Dad was quite a prankster, and that he loved the house we were renting. One night, after we had moved in, I was lying in bed and I smelled smoke. I immediately got up, thinking that the house was on fire, and checked out all the rooms, including the attic, with no evidence of a fire. The smell of smoke seemed to be concentrated in the living room. The very next day we told Tommy about our smoke experience, and then he told us a story about his Dad. One day, his Dad called and said that the house was on fire. Tommy immediately asked where his Mother was. His Dad said: "She is asleep, and I am ready to take a shower". Tommy didn't know whether to believe him or not because his Dad was such a prankster. Thinking it over, he thought it best if he went over to see what was going on. He was amazed to find that there was a small fire in the living room caused by an old fashioned free-standing stove used to heat the house. His Dad was in the shower, his Mother was asleep in the bedroom, and the house was beginning to fill with smoke. Everybody got out safely, and the fire damage was repaired. So, how about my experience smelling smoke! Could it have come from Houston?

As the months passed by, Lovella and I started having unusual experiences, and so did our guests and family members. I will now relate some of these:

- We were keeping our grandson, Ehren, who was 9-months old. We had purchased a crib and a baby monitor a short while before. He hated the crib, and always wanted to be picked up as soon as he awoke. One day, Lovella was in the kitchen cooking our dinner. Suddenly she heard the baby over the monitor starting to cry. At the same time, she heard the voice of someone speaking softly. She thought that, because he quit crying, that it was me. Then, to Lovella's great surprise, I walked in from the outside. She immediately panicked and told me to stand by the monitor and listen. She then rushed to the baby's room. Ehren was sitting in the crib, and unusual for him, was not crying. Lovella grabbed the baby and came back to the kitchen and asked me if I had heard anything on the monitor. I told her that, before she entered the baby's room, I had heard someone speaking in a quiet voice. (WAS IT A FRIENDLY GHOST"?)

- Lovella's oldest son, Juergen, and his wife Jeanie were visiting us one day. That night, they went to bed in our guest room. This was the room Tommy's Dad, Houston, slept in. During the night, they were awakened by the sound of objects falling to the floor. They turned on the lights, and could not believe what they were seeing. On the floor laid a pile of books that had been placed on a sturdy shelf in the clothes closet. There was no way these books could have fallen down by themselves. Both were shaken up by all this, but managed to go back to sleep. Sometime later, they were awakened by the TV set suddenly coming to life. Jeanie said: "Juergen, you are laying on the remote and you must have turned on the TV set"! Juergen replied: "No I am not, Jeanie. The remote is laying on the dresser"! Jeanie then said: "Wooooo! I don't want to sleep in this room"! (GHOST'S AGAIN"?)

- Lovella's youngest son, Dieter, had been staying with us for several months, and was sleeping in this same room. On one occasion, Lovella had to get up during the night to go to the bathroom, and she heard the TV in Dieter's room. She opened the door and found Dieter sound asleep. She then turned the TV off. The next morning she fussed at him for leaving the TV (which was a large unit) on during the night. He then said that he had turned the TV off before going back to sleep. During the night, the TV would come back on, and he had to turn it off. This happened several times that night. This experience, which was similar to Juergen's, repeated several times during his stay with us.

- The most unusual experience in this room happened during a visit by my brother Don. He was in the habit of taking a short nap during the afternoons. Don had been visiting with us one day, and had gone to our guest room for a nap. A few minutes later, he came out with a scared look on his face. He then told us a very strange story. As he was preparing to lay down to go to sleep, all of a sudden he saw his deceased wife, Iris, standing before him with a big smile on her face. The two embraced for a magical moment! Don then asked: "Iris, why did you leave me?" As soon as he uttered those words, she was gone. I should add that my brother was a highly educated person who always had a disbelieving look on his face when we were relating our ghostly experiences. After telling us about Iris, he assured us that he had been wide awake during the whole event. Don wasn't one to get involved with paranormal experiences. That memorable afternoon in his life, Don told us: "I now believe in ghosts!"

- This is the story of a light in the attic. One night, Lovella got up to go to the bathroom. There was a trapdoor to the attic right above the bathroom door. She noticed a light shining through the cracks of the trapdoor. In the hallway, there was a wall switch that operated the attic light. She tried turning the light off, but it kept on shining. The next morning she and her son Dieter climbed up to turn the light off. They then noticed that a light was shining in the far back of the attic. We had never gone that far because of obstructions by large air conditioning ducts, and thus never used that light. Lovella asked Dieter to go back to the light. Dieter asked for a towel to remove the bulb. With great difficulty, he climbed to the back. He looked for a pull chain to turn the light off, but the socket didn't have one. Then to his great surprise, he found that, even though the light was on, it was cold to the touch. The bulb was tight in the socket, but he was able to unscrew it to the point that the light went out. The bulb was a very old bulb. The next day Lovella told Tommy Gollott about the light, telling him that she thought that it was a wiring problem. Two days later, Tommy's electrician showed up to check things out. He went up to the attic to where the light was. He then asked for a light bulb to check out the fixture. Lovella told him there was one already there that Dieter had loosened. The bulb was nowhere to be found. He installed the new bulb and then pulled the chain on the fixture to turn it off. This was the same fixture that Dieter earlier had found not to have a chain. The electrician reported that everything looked OK. A short while later, I went up into the attic and looked around myself to see if the old bulb, by chance, had fallen down after Dieter loosened it. No luck! (HAS ANYONE EVER HEARD OF A GHOST LIGHT"?)

- <u>MYSTERIOUS DOOR OPENINGS</u>
  - In February 2000, I was in Providence Hospital in Mobile, Alabama recovering from triple bypass open-heart surgery. At that time we were operating our "Healthier Food Service" business. We had over 200 customers which included banks, doctors, dentists, auto repair shops, etc. I was the service person who would take snack boxes to these business places. I was also the only salesperson, in a company of 3 people. Lovella served as the office manager, and, together with her sister Freda, would pack the snacks in the boxes. One day, early in February, Freda had just serviced our customers while I was away in the hospital. While she was home alone working on the snack boxes, the front door, which led to a screen porch, opened by itself. At first she thought that she had not closed it properly. She then told us later, that she went and closed the door very firmly. Having done that, she got back to work on the boxes. Suddenly, the door opened again. She then closed it one more time and felt chills running up and down her spine. She continued working on the boxes, while keeping an eye on the door. Again, the door started to open. That was it! She grabbed her purse and said to herself: "I'm out of here"!
  - -Several months went by. One afternoon, Lovella went to the bathroom to take a bath. She was completely undressed waiting for the tub to fill up, when suddenly she saw the doorknob start to turn, and the door slowly open. She yelled: "Al, can't I have any privacy"? There was no answer. She quickly put on a robe and went to the front room. There I was sitting at my computer, while Freda was working on the boxes. She told us about the experience she just had in the bathroom, and then said: "I think Houston must have gotten an eyeful". Then Freda said: "Was Houston laughing"?

○ -Another door opening experience occurred while Dieter was staying with us. There was a door leading from the living room into the snack room. Dieter was a "night owl" and he would close the door so that we would not be disturbed while he watched TV. He would also fix himself something to eat in the adjoining kitchen. One night, he saw the door knob turn, and the door begin to open. He said "Mom! Al!" but nobody answered. Dieter then came to our bedroom and found Lovella sleeping. He woke her up and asked "Where's Al"? Lovella said "He's taking a shower". (Houston Gollott was certainly busy walking around our house that night!)

○ -Another door opening experience occurred while Lovella's niece, Anita, was visiting us with a girlfriend. That night, they told us that they were going out for the evening and would be coming back late. Lovella then told them that she would leave a key to the front door under the entrance floor mat. Upon returning from their midnight outing, they came into the screen porch to the door leading into the house. Anita looked under the floor mat to get the key, and while she was bending over, the door started to open. (That story was our breakfast conversation the next morning).

○ -A final door opening experience: There was a small hallway leading from the work room to the laundry room. On one side there was a half-door that opened up to the house's furnace. One afternoon, Lovella was doing laundry. She left the laundry room and passed by the furnace door and saw that it was open. I was at the computer. Lovella asked: "Why was I looking into the furnace closet"? I told her that I wasn't. We both knew that this half-door would stick and had to be lifted up to open. (Was Houston busy during the day, also?)

• Our Friends' Ghost Stories.

○ One day. Our good friends Ralph and Leda from Oklahoma were visiting us. We had just sat down at our dining table which overlooked beautiful Back Bay. We were discussing some of the unusual happenings that had been occurring in the house recently. I might add that Ralph was retired from a major petroleum company where he held an executive position in the finance department. Being the professional person that he was, Ralph listened to our ghost stories with a half-smile disbelieving look on his face. All of a sudden, he jumped up from his chair and yelled: "Your ghost hit me on the side"! Leda told us that after they returned home to Oklahoma, Ralph would tell everybody about his encounter with a ghost in our house. To add to our ghost stories, Leda and Ralph, many years ago, had experienced a terrible tragedy. They were living in Ponca City, Oklahoma, and it was two weeks before Christmas. Their young 21-year old daughter by the name of Mary Alice, was coming home from college on a Christmas break. She was driving, with a girlfriend riding beside her. It was a snowy afternoon and the road was slippery. Afterwards, it was learned, that for some unknown reason, she hit her brakes. The car immediately went into a spin, and ended up stopped in the opposite lane, with the rear of her car facing oncoming traffic. Suddenly, a pickup truck came up over a rise in the road and hit Mary Alice's car in the rear end. A heart-breaking accident had just occurred! Mary Alice's neck was broken. She passed away on the trip to the hospital. Her girlfriend fortunately was not hurt. Years later, after Ralph and Leda had moved out of the house they lived in at the time the accident occurred, they ran into the new owners. A strange story was told. They related that they saw a young woman who they believed was a ghost, haunting Leda and Ralph's former house.

- At this time, I want to relate a small personal experience. Lovella and I were asleep on our bed, when all of a sudden I was awakened by the rustling of the bedcover over my feet. I turned over and shook Lovella. What was going on? We looked up at the fan over our bed, which was running. Could that be what had moved the blanket? We immediately concluded this couldn't be possible because the bed covering was too heavy, and besides, I had been asleep most of the night, and nothing unusual had happened. In addition, if it had been the fan, it would have continued to rustle the blanket. I might add that the rustling bedcover was experienced several times again.

- People Sightings.
  - Freda was spending the night with us, and all three of us were watching TV. All of a sudden, Freda spoke up and said: "Somebody just walked down the hall. Was it Dieter"? Lovella said "No! Dieter is not here". Freda then said: "I just saw a large man walking down the hall, and I haven't even had a glass of wine"! (Houston, incidentally, was a large man).

  - Another example of somebody seeing a figure happened while Freda's daughter, Anita, and granddaughter, Christa, were visiting us. That evening, Lovella, Anita, Christa, and Dieter were watching TV. All four of them, at the same time, saw a large figure go from the dining room into the hall. Christa then jumped up to her feet and said: "Who was that"? All four agreed that they had seen a large man walking toward the hall.

- Missing Objects.
  - -Lovella was in the kitchen getting ready to prepare some mashed potatoes. She kept a potato masher in the front of a small drawer under the kitchen counter. When she opened the drawer to get the masher, she found that it was missing. At this time, I would like to say that Lovella was known as an organizer. She always knew where she put things. The potato masher had a history of its own. It had belonged to Lovella's Mother who had it until she passed away in 1964. This kitchen utensil meant a lot to Lovella, so not finding it greatly upset her. At that time, three detectives (Lovella, Freda, and Me) formed a "posse" to look for it. Unfortunately, the potato masher was not to be found. The very next morning, Lovella was making breakfast, when she went to the same drawer to get some needed items. To her great shock, there was the potato masher in the same location where it always had been.

  - -In closing this chapter, I want to relate a missing object story that had four very reliable witnesses. In this very "elite" group, we had Lovella, Tommy Gollott, a good neighbor named Bruce, and Me. We had a leak in the dining room ceiling that Tommy and Bruce were repairing. This job required removing several stained acoustic tiles and then cutting some new ones so that they would fit properly in the ceiling. They used a box cutter to do the cutting.

When the job was half-way finished, the knife showed up missing. We then formed our top-rated search team comprised of Lovella, Tommy, Bruce and Me. We searched for a long time. This cracker-jack search team came up with the conclusion that the knife had inadvertently been left on top of one of the tiles during the work process. Tommy then said that he wasn't about to take down the tiles, so I came up with a replacement, and Bruce went home without his knife. Months later, Lovella was putting up Christmas decorations in the dining room. She got up on her stepladder and in plain sight on top of the china cabinet was the famous cutting knife. I might add that from time-to-time, Lovella always dusted the furniture, but never saw the knife. One final piece of evidence was the fact that all four of us looked on top of this cabinet. This episode finally came to an end when we took the knife back to Bruce. As he received it, he smiled and said "He brought it back"!

- -So ends the story of a haunted house. I seriously doubt that any other "Ghost House" has had this many events, told by so many reputable witnesses, over such a long period of time.

- -I must relate a final tragic event. This house was totally destroyed by Hurricane Katrina in the year 2005. Where are these homeless ghosts now??

(More of Katrina and other storms in the next chapter).

CHAPTER 15

BILOXI MISSISSIPPI

I will not attempt to tell the long history of Biloxi, but rather relate some of our experiences while we lived in that city. Most of Biloxi is located south of Interstate 10. Our knowledge of this small Mississippi town was almost non-existent as we traveled over the years on Interstate 10. I remember seeing signs on I-10 inviting the traveler to turn off the highway and head south to what road signs called "The Scenic Route". One day, on one of our travels heading East towards Alabama and Florida, we decided to explore this route and headed south until we came to U.S. Highway 90, which ran East and West, right along the Gulf Of Mexico. On this particular trip, since we were coming from the West, we headed East when we hit Highway 90. As we drove along this stretch of U.S. 90, we began to see beautiful large homes overlooking the Gulf. These homes extended for miles, until we reached the outskirts of Biloxi. Little did we know, at that time, that a major tragedy was awaiting in the future that would end up destroying all of these beautiful mansions. There would be no exceptions. Prior to the advent of casinos, Biloxi's existence rested primarily on its seafood industry, plus a modest tourist trade visiting its beaches.

A major transformation was about to take place that would change everything.

OUR LIFE IN BILOXI

The year was 1994, and we were ready to leave Friendswood, Texas having just sold our little snack business. Our original aim was to head to Florida, where we planned to re-open our food service business. When we reached Mobile, Alabama we made a major change in our plans. Lovella's sister, Freda, and her husband, Fred, lived in Mobile. For a lot of different reasons, (I believe that it was greatly Divine planning), we decided to stay in Alabama and, with help from both Fred and Freda, we restarted our snack business in Mobile. We lived and worked in Mobile for approximately five years. Lovella and I had a travel trailer that we had brought from Texas. We, together with Freda and Fred, made several visits to Biloxi. Shortly thereafter, Lovella and I decided to take our travel trailer to Biloxi and park it near the beach. This trailer ultimately became a week-end get-away for both us and for visiting family members. Towards the end of our activity in Mobile, we had

125

established several accounts in neighboring Mississippi. This opened the door to our next major move. We sold the business in Mobile and started to develop a new business, headquartered in Biloxi. In the previous chapter I described some of the unusual events we experienced in the haunted house we lived in for the following five years. I would now like to describe what "Mother Nature" had planned for our small Mississippi town. I'll start with a major hurricane named Camille. The year was 1969. I'm telling this story about Camille, because it impacted the company I was working for (General Electric) and may have helped me save lives 36 years later. Camille would make history as one of four tropical storms to ever reach a recorded wind speed of 190 miles or more an hour. This category 5 hurricane, starting off the coast of Africa as a tropical wave, would ultimately destroy the Mississippi coast.

The height of the storm surge that would reach the coastline would be 24 feet, and would completely wipe out all building structures as far as 3 to 4 blocks inland. The storm hit the coast during the night of August 17, 1969. At that time, I was working for General Electric in Houston, Texas supporting NASA on the Apollo Moon Program. The Apollo 11 mission had been launched on July 16, and the first landing on the moon had taken place on July 20, 1969. Approximately 1 month later, Camille would make national headlines. On August 18, we received word that a G.E. engineer was reported among eight victims who drowned when the Richelieu Manor Apartments in Pass Christian, Mississippi were destroyed by the giant storm. Reports that a hurricane party was being held at the apartments were never confirmed.

figure 15.1 [76]

HURRICANE CAMILLE

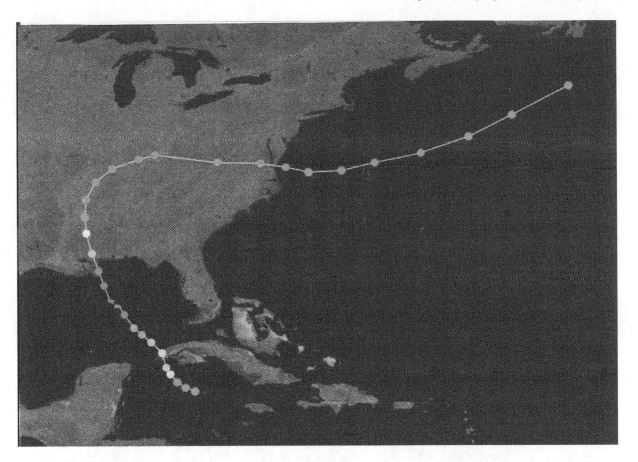

figure 15.2 [77]

PATH OF HURRICANE CAMILLE

figure 15.3 [78]

SHIPS BEACHED IN GULFPORT, MISSISSIPPI

figure 15.4 [79]

THE RICHELIEU MANOR APARTMENTS
(BEFORE CAMILLE)

figure 15.5 [80]

THE RICHELIEU MANOR APARTMENTS
(AFTER CAMILLE)

HURRICANE KATRINA

The year is 2005. The date on the calendar is Monday, August 29. A major hurricane named Katrina would re-write the history of the northern Gulf of Mexico. New Orleans would go under water, and the entire Mississippi coast would be catastrophically destroyed. We had been living in Biloxi for approximately 5 years. In April of 2005, by the Grace of God, we decided to sell our food business and move to Florida. Four months later, the haunted house we had lived in with very happy memories would be completely destroyed by Katrina. If we had not moved, we would have lost all of our belongings and perhaps our lives.

I had been watching, in Florida, the progression of Katrina as it took aim at the Mississippi coast. With all of the Weather Bureau's bulletins pouring in, I became alarmed about the safety of our former neighbors on Bay View Avenue in Biloxi. I decided to call Tommy Gollott and tell him that, for his safety, he should immediately leave Biloxi and head north away from the coast. At this point is where the memory of Hurricane Camille enters the picture. Tommy told me that even though Camille had done serious damage to Biloxi, he had survived that category 5 storm. He went on to relate that the 1969 storm had flooded Biloxi, and that he had seen his dining room table float out to the Back Bay. Nevertheless, he went on to remind me, that the large mansion that had just been completed and where he was planning to ride the storm out, was built many times stronger that his former house. Having seen him build the new house, I can understand why Tommy had so much trust in its structural integrity. I told him, however, that I still had a foreboding about the coming storm, and pleaded with him to leave Biloxi. He ultimately left, thank the Good Lord, and went to a relative's house many miles away north from the coast, where he and his family would be safe. The next morning, Katrina came ashore with a 30-foot wall of water. It was around 6 A.M. Central Time. The devastation was complete. Most of the houses in our old neighborhood were wiped out. This included the house we had been living in, together with Tanya's (our landlady next door) two story Victorian house. Absolutely nothing remained of our former house. When we visited the area around Christmas, a strange survival had taken place. Although Tanya's house had totally disappeared, Lovella had walked over to where it had stood for many years and found the remains of three figurines. They were the famous three monkeys: "See No Evil; Hear No Evil; and Speak No Evil". They had been sitting on top of Tanya's refrigerator. It and the two-story house were gone, and yet the three little monkeys were still there, although damaged, on the ground.

We then went over to Tommy's house. The wall of water had rushed through the bottom floor, carrying away all of the kitchen appliances and counters, breaking all of the windows, and blowing out the large double front door. Because of their geometry, the large white columns survived. Tommy showed us the water mark on the inside walls. It was around 7 feet. The house still stood!

Most of the neighborhood was gone. A house a couple of blocks away was destroyed, and a large Vietnamese family that had been living there were all drowned. Lovella spoke to a neighbor not far away from the Gollott's house. They told her that when the storm was on top of them, they had time to climb a large tree nearby and tie themselves to it with ropes. As the wall of water went by, they saw what they thought was a tornado, pick up a neighbor's guest house, and spin it off to where it exploded in the air. (They said that it reminded them of Dorothy's house in "The Wizard Of Oz").

figure 15.6 [81]

HURRICANE KATRINA (AUGUST 28, 2005)

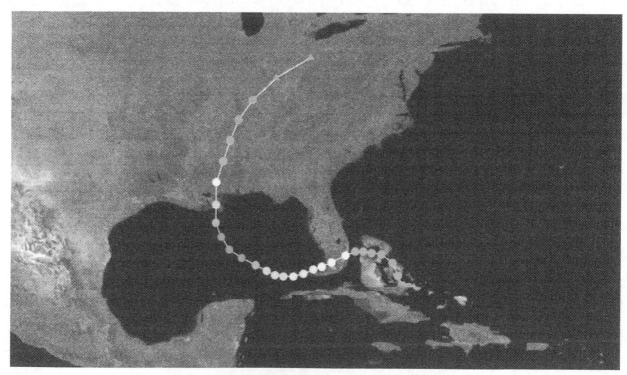

figure 15.7 [82]

STORM TRACK OF HURRICANE KATRINA

figure 15.8 [83]

OUR HOUSE BEFORE KATRINA

figure 15.9 [84]

WHERE OUR HOUSE STOOD AFTER KATRINA

figure 15.10 [85]

TANYA'S HOUSE BEFORE KATRINA

figure 15.11 [86]

TANYA'S HOUSE AFTER KATRINA, TOMMY'S HOUSE TO LEFT

CHAPTER 16

ADDICTIONS

The world is full of addictions. It is safe to say that there are very few people that don't have an addiction. An addiction can be defined as anything that becomes an obsession to the exclusion of everything else. It is basically very selfish and is primarily enjoyed by one's self. Another characteristic of addictions is that you don't want to discuss it with anyone else, and actually resent anybody questioning your obsession. The reason for this is that you enjoy your addiction, and the last thing on your mind is having to defend it. There are countless types of addictions. The big four are: (1) Drugs (including prescription drugs); (2) Alcohol; (3) Smoking; and (4) Gambling. Not far behind these four are: (5) Food; (6) Money; (7) Sleep; (8) Power; (9) Sex; (10) Fame; (11) Work; (12) Reading; (13) Computers; and the list goes on.

Among our relatives and friends, there are several examples of The Big Four. I am not going to pursue this in my story to avoid discussing this sensitive subject about those near us. I will, however, tell a story about me and my life companion. The year was 1999, and we had moved from Mobile, Alabama to Biloxi, Mississippi. While in Mobile, Lovella and I started our small snack business, which we had originally started in Friendswood, Texas. The business in Mobile grew to the point that we decided to sell it. As related earlier in this narrative, we had started to sell to customers in Mississippi. When we sold the Mobile business, this left us with a "starter" business in Mississippi. We had become acquainted with Biloxi and its gambling temptations through many previous week-end trips. This was a strong enough attraction for us to open up our new business in Biloxi, the so-called "sin city" on the Mississippi Gulf Coast.

We spent many happy years in Biloxi, enjoying the beaches, the excellent seafood cuisine, and our "haunted house". Many relatives and friends would come to visit us, in part attracted by the city's entertainment. The years went by, and we slowly succumbed to Biloxi's temptations. Although we always met our financial obligations, the local night life was using up too much of our material resources. A financial stress was developing, to the point that we contemplated going to a lawyer and discuss the possibility of declaring Chapter 7 Bankruptcy. To those unfamiliar with the legalities of bankruptcy, Chapter 7 enables a person to discharge all financial obligations. The only exception one usually made, for obvious reasons, was the financing of an automobile. There is a big downside to all of this. One's credit rating hits rock bottom. Financial institutions such as banks don't forgive you for at least seven to ten years. The irony of bankruptcy is that large corporations such as airlines, auto manufacturers and countless other business enterprises use this strategy to get out of financial commitments, too often to the detriment of the small investor. Well, so much for rationalizing one's own shortcomings!

Now comes the interesting part of this sad story. Lovella and I got involved in something whose scope had never been duplicated by few, if any other person.

Most all casinos have a credit system they call "markers". As long as you have a good bank account, you can borrow gambling money. This money must be covered by your bank two weeks later. Some people use this system to gamble large amounts of money. In our case, the money we drew out was substantial, but not exorbitant. At least we didn't think so. We started to draw out $1000, hoping, like all good gamblers do, that we would be able to double our money. This idea is a joke. Very smart business men plan the operation of a casino just to take your money. They will give some money back as you play to keep you hoping, but sooner or later, they will always take it back. The hope that you might be the exception to this trap is a pipe dream. The best way to realize this is to look at their beautiful palaces that were all built with "loser's" money. As our finances deteriorated, markers became an easy way to get money. The catch, however, was that doubling our money never seemed to work out. All of a sudden, the two-week loan grace period was up. What to do? The obvious answer was to go to another casino and draw out a new marker. To pay that marker we then decided that we both should get markers. The amount involved in this nightmare game grew to $15,000. This large sum of money required both of us to obtain markers daily to cover the other casino markers. We ended up not gambling with any of this money. THE DOWNWARD SPIRAL HAD STARTED. When we finished going down this disastrous road, we had $1000 commitments to every major casino in Biloxi. Out of 10 casinos on the Mississippi Gulf Coast, we had played the "marker game" on 8 of them. Some of these casinos were owned by the "Big Boys" in Las Vegas.

Bankruptcy then became the only way out. We immediately went to a bankruptcy lawyer and discussed the whole sad story. At this time I should mention the "Big Elephant" in the room. If we included the money owed to the casinos, what might happen to us if we were confronted by big-time lawyers from some of the largest casinos in the world? Would the "Big Boys", as in the movies, break our legs? Our lawyer couldn't guarantee it, but he felt that the casinos would not take us to court. This would result in bad publicity for them. Fortunately, our lawyer was right, and all of our debts, including those owed to the casinos were discharged. The date was April 2003. We were told by the bankruptcy court that details of our case would remain on our credit report for 10 years. Three years after our bankruptcy, however, by some miracle from Above, we were able to purchase a new minivan, which was essential to our business. What lay ahead for the casinos was a disaster by the name of Hurricane Katrina. The storm did tremendous damage to most of the casinos. Since casinos, by law at that time had to be on the water, they were all built on huge barges. Katrina gutted some of them, and washed across Highway 90 a few others. Only one of the 10 casinos would be able to re-open in a short period of time. Two others re-opened late in the year. The rest would take one or more years to come back to life.

Did we learn a lesson from all this? That story remains to be told in another book!

CHAPTER 17

THE POWER OF PRAYER

For those who believe and trust in God, they could write a book or books covering a life-time of prayer. I will illustrate this subject with a few examples, primarily for those who either do not believe, or who vacillate between belief and unbelief.

The year was 1937. This is an example of prayer helping to resolve a major family crisis. My sister Ruth and my sister Peggy were walking along a street when Ruth, all of a sudden, started to experience severe pain in her lower right side. When they rushed home, Dad believed that it was probably her appendix. He had a large medical dictionary that someone had given him. In the dictionary, he read that one attack, followed by a second incident did not require immediate hospitalization. Ruth and Peggy later went to downtown Buenos Aires, Argentina to attend a singing rehearsal in a church choir. Ruth remembers that the hymn was "Be Still My Soul". Afterwards, they were both walking away from the church, when all of a sudden Ruth experienced a 2nd attack of pain, again, in her lower right side. They then knew that something was very wrong. Ruth was 16 years old at the time. What they didn't know was that Ruth's appendix had ruptured and her life was in immediate danger. It was early evening and Mother and Dad were already in bed.

They rushed home, and Peggy woke them up, yelling that something had to be done. Mother later told us that by that time, Ruth had collapsed. Her body was in shock, and she appeared lifeless. They immediately rushed her to the British Hospital, where the emergency room doctor told Mother and Dad that they only had 20 minutes to save her life. She was quickly wheeled to the operating room and was prepared for an immediate operation. At that time, ether was used to sedate patients. There was danger, however, in the use of ether, Mother and Dad were told, and it might kill her. Fortunately, (and I believe with help from Above) the hospital the day before had introduced a new anesthetic gas that was much safer. Ruth by this time had lost all of her color and her body was turning cold. The operation turned out to be successfull, but it took her 18 days to recover in the hospital. The night of the operation, Mother told me that she and Dad stayed on their knees until dawn, praying to God that Ruth's life be spared. The story has a happy ending. The fervent prayers of a mother and father were answered, and I ended up with a great sister.

This next story involves my sister Ann's missionary daughter, Debbie, together with her husband Todd and their three children, Sully, Emily, and Baby Jordan. Debbie, Todd and their children were working as missionaries in Mali, Africa. Mali is a landlocked country with a 90% Muslim population, in northwest Africa. It borders, and in fact, includes a large area of the Sahara desert. Their oldest child was a boy by the name of Sully. The little family was taking a vacation using a new car, their first, furnished by the Christian and Missionary Alliance. In the car, were Debbie,Todd, Sully, Emily,and Baby Jordan in a child's seat. They stopped for gas at a small store. Debbie and Emily got out to go to the bathroom. As they walked into the store, Todd had just got back in the car when several hijackers appeared with guns drawn. They threw Todd out with force, and took off with the two children still in the car. Todd immediately jumped on the back of the car, and was able to hold on to the spare tire as it sped off. He found himself desperately holding on to the careening car. He started yelling "Give me my children"! At that moment, one of the gunmen stuck a gun out of the window and yelled to Todd: "Do you want to die"? Meanwhile, back at the store, Debbie, witnessing with horror at what was happening, immediately asked: "Are there any Christians here"? At that moment, Debbie and three women in the store got down on their knees and began to pray fervently for the safety of the family. All of a sudden, after the hijacked car had gone about two miles, it suddenly stopped. The hijackers then released the children into the arms of Todd, and sped off at a high rate of speed. The car was never found, but the miraculous thing in this story was that Todd and the children were unhurt. What a wonderful illustration of the power of prayer!

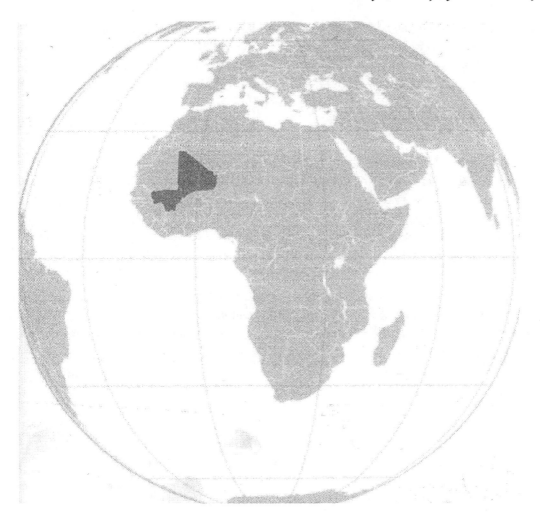

figure 17.1 [87]

THE REPUBLIC OF MALI

(Area shown in dark gray on the map of Africa)

A third example is less dramatic, but might be of interest to those who are still not convinced. The year was 1962. Phiddy (my late wife) and I had just moved from Baltimore, Maryland to Syracuse, New York. As I related in an earlier chapter, I had accepted a job with General Electric after having worked for Westinghouse Electric for 10 years. The time was early spring. We had just driven up with our dog named Snoopy, and our two Siamese cats named Chops and Suey. Phiddy and I were fortunate to find a house we could rent, situated on a hill overlooking the entire city of Syracuse. After the long trip from Baltimore, we were happy to have found a place in our new home where we could house our three pets. A litter box was provided for our cats, and as for Snoopy, he would get regular walks looking for fire hydrants. After a week had passed, we felt that our animals were sufficiently acclimated to their new surroundings to enable me to install a "doggy door" leading to our fenced back yard. Everything went well for one or two weeks, when one morning, I counted noses, and came up with one short. After a quick roll call, I was able to identify the missing pet. It was Chops, our blue point Siamese male cat.

What followed was three days of frantic searching in the neighborhood, all to no avail. Phiddy and I were very attached to our pets, and considered them part of our family. I tried to console her, without much success. She said that she would pray that Chops had found a good home. To ease the pain, I told her that I would put an ad in the paper saying that we had lost our cat. The ad was placed on a Monday and ran for a week until the following Sunday. A week later we had not heard from anyone on our missing cat. Two days later, our phone rings. A lady with a friendly voice said that she had spotted our ad. The story she told was that she had seen a strange cat in the woods back of her house. She was an avid bird lover, and was afraid that the cat might do harm to her feathered friends. She described the cat, and her description seemed to match our missing Siamese cat. Overjoyed, Phiddy and I drove for about 10 to 15 miles to the lady's house. There, to our great delight, was our missing Chops. The story then got interesting. The lady told us that after she read the Sunday paper, by evening, she would throw it in the trash to be picked up the following day. For some reason, (I think prayer was the answer), this time she had not thrown away the paper. She started to thumb through the large Sunday paper for a reason she can't explain. She opened the newspaper to the want ads and there was our missing cat ad. The interesting thing was that this was Tuesday afternoon, long after the Sunday paper was usually discarded. One other part of this story is that Chops had headed east to the fringe of the New York Thruway. This was the highway that we took to come to Syracuse from Baltimore, a total of 260 miles, with New York City in the way. What a trip that would have been for Chops, as he tried to return to our former home in Baltimore. Prayer was surely answered!

Prayer is the acknowledgement that God exists. It is also comforting to have someone to pray to, knowing that He only has love towards you. I'll close this chapter with these three stories, but, I might add, there are countless numbers of answered prayers awaiting me in my life ahead.

CHAPTER 18

DOES GOD EXIST?

I'll say from the beginning a resounding YES, God does exist. People have sought to know Him since the dawn of time. For true believers, there is ample evidence of His existence. These include miracles and healings without number, daily consoling and guidance, inspiration, creation itself, and above all others, "LOVE, MERCY, & FORGIVENESS". There are many attributes that define God to me. Above all others, I believe that He is the only creator. For those poor souls who do not believe in God, they have lost their way and live in darkness. In Psalms, Chapter 14, verse 1, we find the words: "The fool has said in his heart: There is no God"!

Several years ago I had a miraculous event to occur. This experience proved to be the most blessed event in my life and gave me absolute proof of God's existence. I go back thirty plus years to the early 70's. I was living in a small town near NASA's Johnson Space Center, south of Houston, Texas. It was early evening. In those years, I was involved with a small group that used to meet to discuss esoteric subjects. We all practiced meditation as a means of communicating with our "higher selves". That evening I did something that I had never done before. I lit a small scented candle. Then I took my Bible and started reading aloud from the book of Psalms, beginning with the first Psalm. When I reached the 25th Psalm, I stopped. I then closed my eyes in meditation. A few moments later, I distinctly heard an inner voice uttering a short phrase of praise to God. The voice then asked me to repeat it. Then I was asked a 2nd and 3rd time. As soon as I finished, I saw the Earth as a slate gray disc, without any noticeable features. At that very moment, I felt that I personally loved every individual on Earth. This sense of love was literal and true. The moment lasted for a split second, and then I heard what sounded like a "ping". That was the end of my experience. The only answer that comes to me, is that for a split second, I became united with God, for only God could express this universal love. The slate gray disc was, perhaps, God wiping mankind's "slate" clean. Just like a mother loves her child, even though it may turn out to be bad in later life, so God still loves His original creation that was pure and perfect.

A belief in God can be based either solely on faith, or the belief in the Bible, or after an examination of all that is around us. I would like to elaborate on the latter by describing the world we live in:

- First of all, we are just the right distance from the sun to receive the warmth that we need to exist.

- The Earth is tilted in its axis to provide us with a change in seasons.

- We have an atmosphere that provides us with essential oxygen to survive. This same atmosphere protects us from damaging solar radiation, and objects that enter our atmosphere but are quickly destroyed by re-entry heat.

- The plants of the world use the carbon dioxide we exhale as a waste gas, and using sunlight and water, convert it into food through a process called "photosynthesis". They then release our precious oxygen as a by-product. What a beautiful concept.

- Approximately 70% of the earth's surface is covered by water. These oceans generate our weather systems, while supplying us with boundless sources of food.

- Mankind needs fuel to provide him with warmth. Initially, this was possible using wood. Then came the discovery of coal. This was followed by the discovery of petroleum and natural gas. After that came nuclear energy. Scientists forecast that in the future we may be able to take hydrogen from water and re-create the energy used by our Sun.

- This wonderful world supplies us with animals that provide us with food, clothing and beasts of burden.

- The plant world gives us both food and products that we can use to make clothing and shelter.

I could go on and on, page after page, presenting the wonders of our world. And I haven't mentioned the most wonderful creation of all, mankind.

How can any intelligent person not see God's Divine Plan unfolding before their very eyes? To say that all of this was created from nothing and evolved by accidental and coinciding events is pure idiocy.

A final thought on the subject of God's existence. From the beginning, all of mankind has sensed the need to look for a Divine Presence to explain their existence and purpose. To many, this yearning to know a Divine Creator is proof enough of God's existence.

POSCRIPT

I've hesitated to add this section to my chapter on God. I am doing it because of an article by a professor at a mid-western University. Not long ago, he wrote an article in a national newspaper that stated that religion and science are hopelessly incompatible. I read this article and decided that it was a major arrow aimed at the heart of religion. This professor is a totally dedicated advocate of atheism. As an ex-aerospace engineer, I've lived in a world where everything had to be viewed in a scientific and logical way. Problems were only solved by taking in solid and concrete facts. There was no room for theoretical approaches. With this background, I analyzed the professor's dissertation and found it wanting in many ways. I sent him an E-mail stating my analysis of his article. I might add that I never heard from him. I would like to present some of the dialogue from my article:

First of all, as an engineer I was taught that there is no such thing as "Perpetual Motion" and that in science, everything has a beginning and an end. Since the current most popular belief on the origin of the Universe starts with the "Big Bang Theory", where did the initial "Super Atom" that initiated the evolution of the Universe come from? As a Christian, I believe that God created the "Super Atom". After all, you can't create something from nothing. God then established a set of universal laws that would result and control the evolution of the Universe. I thus believe in the Theory of Evolution. I believe that the whole Universe, including our planet and everything on it, is evolving in accordance with these universal laws. So where is the confrontation with religion? It solely rests with the creation of Man. What science doesn't comprehend is that Man was created as a spiritual being. Science is not able to prove or disprove something that started out as a non-physical being. God, the creator of both the physical and spiritual worlds, introduced man fully developed and equipped with the mental capacity to develop and evolve the society we now know. The professor quotes about an investigation of the brain to see if scientists can detect the evidence of a soul. Can science find evidence of LOVE, HATE, FRIENDSHIP, INSPIRATION, etc. in the brain? He went on to discuss evil and the Holocaust as examples that God doesn't exist. In other words, how can a loving God let these things happen? The answer lies in our spiritual creation. When we were created, God gave us two great gifts. First and foremost, He gave us life; but secondly, and equally important, He gave us free will. We then were free to choose between good and evil. In this case, I believe that evil is the disobedience of God's universal laws. This is like a child being told by his parents not to do certain things, but when they do it, bad things happen. If God interceded every time something evil was happening, where would be our free will?

I then wrote the professor about a recorded story that proves the existence of a non-physical world. This was written by a doctor who described a blind man who passed away on a hospital table. Even though he had suffered cardiac arrest, the doctors continued to work on him. A short while later, they were able to resuscitate him. The blind man, (from birth, I might add), told an amazing story. He found himself floating above his body. When he came to, he described in detail the room and all those who were in the room. A blind man? This illustrates the difference between the mind and the brain.

A final word: Does the good professor really believe that we are only intelligent animals that will live for a few short years, and then become dust, never to be known as having ever existed?

CHAPTER 19

WHERE DID WE COME FROM?

To many, this is a question that cannot be answered. I believe, however, that asking this question and seeking an answer can lead us to a better understanding of who we are, and how we fit into the plan of creation.

I believe that we are both physical and spiritual beings. We all know how our physical bodies came into existence. What we don't know is how the spiritual part of our being came to be. Since I believe that God created us in His image, we are in truth spiritual beings, and as such, immortal. The question that no one seems to ask is this. If God created us as spiritual beings, when did this take place? It is totally unreasonable that God is on "standby" to create souls as soon as a man and woman jump into bed. Does that mean that there is a storage place where billions of souls are waiting for a human body to be created, many times accidentally? Such thoughts are preposterous, and no amount of pondering on this subject seems to provide us with a reasonable answer. Yet there is another answer. What if we pre-existed in another life. There is evidence in the Bible that this is true. One of the best known can be found in Jeremiah, Chapter 1, verses 4 & 5. Jeremiah is speaking: "Now the word of the Lord came to me saying: Before I formed you in the womb I knew you, and before you were born, I consecrated you". These words strongly imply that we existed before our bodies developed in the womb. I believe that we were created before time began. At that moment of creation, God gave us two great gifts: Life and free will. Our spirits were created pure and perfect, and we have to believe that we had individual identity. In all probability, God named each one of us.

Before going in this new direction, let us consider how many souls we are talking about. The current population of the world is approximately 7 billion, and growing. It is reasonable to assume that, except for a small number, all 7 billion people currently living on this planet will have crossed over to the other side in 100 years. Working the math, that comes out to an average of 70 million people that pass away each year. Taking this forward, we end up with close to 200,000 dying every day. That is a lot of souls daily leaving this planet. One other fact we need to take into consideration is that there are substantially more people being born than people passing away. The road to the next life is indeed very heavily traveled.

Why am I bringing up all these numbers? We need to try to understand the very complex story of Man's creation. If God was still creating over 200,000 souls a day, the Bible would not have said that God had finished his creation, and was therefore resting. He still would be kept very busy creating new souls.

We must, first of all, realize that biologically, the human race is part of the animal kingdom, the warm-blooded mammal branch. The life that a pregnant woman feels in her womb is undoubtedly felt by other members of our animal branch. There are, however, two distinct and marvelous differences. Firstly, we are way superior in our intelligence, but most importantly, we are the only species that has a soul. A perennial question that comes up, particularly during presidential elections, is when does human life begin? As noted earlier, life obviously begins at conception. Admitting that the pregnant woman does not create a soul, when may I ask, does our God-created spirit enter into the body? The question is unanswerable. We can, however, consider why we are here on Earth. I believe that the purpose of this life is to develop both mentally and spiritually, and through this journey, to experience the many emotional encounters we all have daily. Additionally, and most importantly for our spiritual development, to choose between good and evil, between right and wrong in all the many experiences we encounter in our lifetime. The soul cannot begin to fulfill this purpose in the womb. It is possible, therefore, that the soul enters the body at birth.

A final thought on this subject. If human life, complete with a soul, begins at conception, then we are faced with the prospect of formal burials, including religious services, for the embryos discarded by miscarriages. This could apply to almost microscopic matter right after conception. I, for one, cannot imagine these funeral services. Deep in my soul I have an unusual memory. I see myself in an opening in the clouds looking down on Earth. I am speaking to someone beside me. I'm saying: "I am about to be born". I have always thought, when having this strange memory, that the person I was speaking to might be my future younger brother, Don, who wouldn't be born for another 4 years.

CHAPTER 20

SIGNS FROM ABOVE

Along life's journey, we many times encounter events that defy all simple explanations. These occurrences happen uniquely with each one of us, and never seem to be shared with anyone else. It is as if they are meant only for us. In this chapter, I am going to relate four events that fall into this category. The purpose in telling these stories is to open our minds that there are other things happening in our lives that may not only provide us with comfort, but in sharing these stories, may lead others in looking into their own lives for unexplainable events. The more we look at some of these events, the more our eyes and minds will be open to other possibilities beyond our ordinary every-day living.

The first experience I am going to relate involves a dove. I was working on the roof of a large shed in back of the house we were leasing in Biloxi, Mississippi. I climbed a ladder with a large bucket of white paint. As I stepped out on the roof, I had a very strong uneasy feeling. The shoes I wore were not providing me with a sure footing. I felt that I was in danger of falling. I was thinking of stopping the painting and climbing back down to the ground. All of a sudden, I noticed a dove perched on a nearby limb that hung over one side of the roof. Not wanting to disturb my little feathered friend, I moved to another part of the roof. As I started to paint, I was again overwhelmed with a feeling of danger. Then to my great surprise, the dove flew to a branch near me. I felt the eyes of the dove looking down on me. At this point, I would like to say that doves are very shy creatures, and usually travel in pairs. There is no reason a dove would perch itself that close to me, and all by itself.

By this time, I felt very insecure, and decided to come down from the roof. Was this unusual event sent down to me to protect me from harm? When I told this story to my wife, Lovella, she said that the dove may have been sent to me by my Mother, who had passed away several years before, to warn me of impending danger.

The second story I wish to relate also involved a dove. It was February 2nd (ground hog day) of the New Year 2000, and also the beginning of the 21st century. That day, while Lovella and I were taking a short walk, I began to experience chest pains and nausea. Without further discussion, Lovella said:

"We are taking you to the hospital"! At that time, we were living in our Biloxi rented house. I told her that I would be all right, but the pain persisted. Lovella then said: "We are going to Mobile, Alabama", which was about 60 miles away. We both knew that in Mobile was a highly rated hospital called, interestingly, Providence Hospital. I was immediately rushed to the emergency room. After a very brief examination, I was wheeled to a nearby room. The doctor that examined me quickly ordered a heart catherization. To those unfamiliar with this procedure, it involves inserting a probe, with an attached very small camera, into a main artery in my groin area. All this was done under general anesthesia. During the procedure, the doctor examined my heart arteries looking for plaque buildup obstructing blood flow into my heart. During the exam, I went into shock, and my wife was told that I had to have open-heart surgery the next day. Shortly thereafter, I came out of my anesthetic sleep, and, since I had not eaten any food that day, I asked for some food. When the food arrived, as soon as I started eating, I went into shock again. The attending physician said that I would immediately have to go into surgery. Fortunately, (and I should say, by Divine Providence), a heart surgeon was available. As they wheeled me down the corridor, I heard Lovella, who was running alongside, say: "Don't leave me Al". I don't remember much else until I awoke many hours later in the intensive care unit. During all of this, Lovella went to the waiting room to await word from my surgery. Feeling all alone, she went to a nearby window and looked out. There, to her great surprise, sat a lonely dove on a ledge four stories up. She felt the gaze of the dove as she looked out. The dove stood on the ledge for all of the time that I was in surgery. After a long wait, a nurse came in and said that they were re-starting my heart, which had been stopped during the surgery. Incidentally, the heart operation took approximately four hours, during which time blood was being pumped through my body by a "heart-lung" machine. The nurse then asked Lovella if she had family members that she could call to keep her company. To Lovella, this sounded like I had passed away. Her sister Freda and husband Fred were out of town, but from earlier visits, they got to know one of their neighbors, Claude and Lillian. Not knowing anyone else to go to, she called and told them about what happened to me in the hospital. When her friends arrived, they were discussing the day's events, when Lovella all of a sudden looked out the window and saw that her friendly dove was gone. She started to cry as she told her friends the story of the dove. The two friends then said: "We are here now, and you don't need the dove anymore". Lovella inwardly gave thanks to God for sending, what she believed, was a comforting sign. I can end this narrative by saying that the operation was successful, and the Good Lord gave me a new lease on life.

This is another hospital story involving yours truly. The year was 2006, and we were living in a small town called Humble, just north of Houston, Texas. That morning, I suddenly, for unknown reasons, felt chest pains. Lovella, knowing my past history with my heart, immediately said: "We are going to the hospital"! Approximately 10 miles away, there was a hospital called Memorial Hermann. It was part of a very large hospital in downtown Houston. Lovella rushed me to the emergency entrance. The doctor in ER examined me and immediately ordered that I be admitted to the hospital where I was taken to a private room. In the meantime, my heart doctor had been called. Upon examining me, he scheduled a heart catherization to be performed the next day. This was the same procedure I had in Providence Hospital, Mobile, Alabama, 6 years before. When the time came the next morning for me to have my examination, a nurse came in and injected, through the IV in my arm, a strong anesthetic solution. This is a shot that is normally given to a patient so that he becomes totally unaware of what was going on. Lovella called it the "I don't care" shot. She had the same procedure performed 2 or 3 weeks earlier in the same hospital. As she watched the nurse give me the shot directly into my IV, she said: "You are lucky. I was given the shot in the part of my body you normally sit down on". This part of the body is popularly known as "the butt". It is also known by other names, but it would be inappropriate for me to use these vulgar terms in my book.

As soon as Lovella made this comment, a strange look came over the face of the nurse. Lovella, at that moment, felt that the nurse had done something wrong. A male nurse then entered my room with a wheel chair to take me down to the catherization lab. By that time, I had grown limp, and the male attendant had trouble getting me into the wheelchair. He asked "Why is he so out of it"? Lovella then told him what the nurse had done when she injected the shot directly into my IV. The male nurse immediately exclaimed: "Oh no"! I was then rushed down to the catherization lab. Lovella followed me and went to an adjoining waiting room. The room was full of people waiting to hear about their loved ones. Lovella had been told that the procedure would not take more than one hour. Time dragged by, and several hours had passed. The waiting room began to empty out, and suddenly Lovella found herself alone. She got up and went into the hall where there was a large window. Hoping, without success, to find someone that she could talk to and get some news of what was happening to me, she went to the window and looked down on a small courtyard. There, to her great surprise, she saw a small dove. Her mind immediately went back several years to my open-heart surgery, and remembered the little dove on the ledge. Could this be a sign, she thought, that had been sent to her to let her know that she was being watched over? It should be noted that the window was right across from the waiting area. All of a sudden a very tall African-American woman, with a beautiful kind face, came up to her and asked: "Are you all right"? At that moment, Lovella broke down and started to cry. She told the black lady that her husband had been taken to the catherization lab, and had been gone for a long time. The black lady then took Lovella by the hand into the waiting room. There, Lovella saw four more black ladies. All five were very tall with kind faces. The first black lady told the other ladies that Lovella was worried about her husband, because the procedure was taking too long. The other four ladies then stood up and formed a circle with Lovella. All five and Lovella held hands in the circle.

The ladies then began to pray in what sounded like a chant. Lovella couldn't understand a word. During this prayer, she started to feel relieved and she felt a warm sensation taking hold of her. The chanting suddenly stopped, and the lady that took her into the waiting room said: "Your husband is going to be all right"! In the meantime, I was lying on the examining table, when suddenly I came to. My doctor was pushing the scope up my artery, and I was beginning to feel what was happening to me. I remember asking: "Are you almost finished"? The doctor answered that he was almost done. Later, after the procedure was finished, the doctor came to the door of the waiting room, and motioned to Lovella to follow him to another room. There he explained that the nurse had made a mistake with the anesthesia. He went on to say that although he had encountered some problems during the examination, everything worked out satisfactorily. He then apologized to Lovella for the nurses error in giving me the anesthesia shot directly into my IV. He explained to Lovella that putting the anesthesia directly into the IV resulted in an immediate and strong reaction. Unfortunately, the anesthesia would weaken before the heart catherization was completed. This is exactly what happened to me in the cath lab. Lovella then went back to the main waiting room to tell the black ladies that I was going to be OK. To her astonishment, the room was completely empty. Lovella later told me that she never saw them entering the room or leaving the room. Could this be visitations from the other side sent to her to provide comfort?

The Life Journey of a Missionary's Son

One final hospital story: Lovella's brother, Randall, had become very ill in Mobile, Alabama while he was visiting his sister, Freda. There was a large Veterans Administration hospital located in Gulfport, Mississippi. Randall, being a veteran, was taken to the hospital, which was about 70 to 80 miles west of Mobile. Randall, for years had suffered from diabetes, and had been taking insulin twice a day. After the doctors examined him, they found a serious infection in his right leg which caused poor circulation in that limb. This problem was a common occurrence with severe diabetics. Knowing that a critical operation would be required to save his leg, they determined that it would be better if he were transferred to a much larger and better equipped VA hospital in Houston, Texas. This long trip of about 450 miles would be done by ambulance. Randall remained in the Houston VA hospital for about 2 weeks. During his stay there, several doctors, having very specialized skills, operated on his leg. They had to remove part of his infected foot, and then replaced several major arteries. This procedure saved his leg from amputation. In the meantime, to add a further burden on the family, I was having major problems of my own. The timing was unfortunate, but my heart suddenly started acting up. I began to have strong pains in my chest. Lovella immediately took me to St. Luke's Hospital in downtown Houston. This hospital was world-wide known for its excellence in the medical field. I soon found out that I had suffered a mild heart attack. My greatest fear was that I would have to undergo a second heart by-pass procedure.

Fortunately, again, the highly experienced doctors avoided this by inserting stents in two of my clogged arteries. During the following week, while I was recovering from my operation at home, Randall had undergone his artery replacement procedure. The operation having been successfully completed, the Houston VA Hospital decided to transfer him once again by ambulance back to Mobile where he would be closer to his home. Lovella and I decided to visit him before the transfer. It was a dark and stormy day, so Lovella asked me to do the driving. We then had a very pleasant visit with Randall. During the visit, he was sitting on the side of his bed with his back to a large window. Lovella and I were both sitting facing the window. Since I was still recovering from my operation, I started to doze in my chair. All of a sudden, Lovella noticed dark clouds moving outside the window. She was concerned about the approaching storm. Suddenly the clouds mysteriously opened up, forming a perfect arch. To her utter amazement, she saw the outline of a figure looking down into the room. It was a figure of Jesus. She tried to wake me up to see this extraordinary scene, but was unsuccessful. When I finally woke up, the cloud formation had disappeared. Nothing was said to Randall about what had just happened. We then said what would turn out to be our final farewells, and headed back to our home in Humble. As we were driving north on the freeway, a postscript was added to the day's event. There in front of us was a car with the words "GO RANDALL" on the license plate frame. All these experiences were vividly brought back to mind when we heard that Randall had passed away the following day.

147

CHAPTER 21

PREDESTINATION AND FREE WILL

Countless books have been written on these subjects, and I have no intention of delving into them just to present my personal beliefs. With my background in engineering, I was taught to examine cause and effect to arrive at a solution to a problem. This will guide me in the following discussion.

I would first like to present what are generally considered the four major religions of the world. They are, in order of their size:

- Christianity : 2.2 billion
- Islam : 1.3 billion
- Hinduism : 900 million
- Buddhism : 360 million

These numbers in no way identify pure and consecrated followers of these religions. If we apply rigid dogmas, few would qualify for the label. In all of these religions, however, most of the members of these groups believe in a Supreme Deity, or God.

Who or what determines where you are born? The answer will decide what is going to be your belief in God. The same question can be applied to the world's population as a whole. In this case, how long you live and what will be the quality of your life will be determined on your place of birth. Again, who or what decides the place of your birth? I personally believe in a merciful God who represents both perfect love and perfect justice. I also believe we were given the great gift of free will when we were created by God. How do we explain being born into poverty, disease, starvation, war? Why are some of us fortunate enough to be born into wealthy families, while others are born into poor families? Why do some of us live a short life, sometimes not outgrowing infancy, while others live to a ripe old age? Why were some of us born during the Dark Ages or in Mongolia during the terrible reign of Genghis Kahn, while others were born in the United States with all of its opportunities? I could go on and on with countless examples of this inequality of birth. Since I firmly believe in free will, and a loving God, we must have had life experiences at other times and places. Having free will, means that we must have been involved in the planning of our present lives. The quality of our present lives must have been predicated on previous experiences. If you don't believe this, then you believe in "the roll of the dice". Bad luck! Who, you might ask, would choose to be born into poverty and disease, or even mental deficiency? From a religious standpoint, can a soul in a mentally deficient body with a mentality of a five-year old be held accountable for its spiritual growth? To try to answer this question, I am going to relate how choices are presented through life's education. If we only attend school through the elementary grades, our choices in what we become are very limited. As we expand our education to the middle school, high school and college level, our available choices in life's work expand proportionally. If we continue through post graduate studies, our horizon becomes almost unlimited. We were created as both physical and spiritual beings. I believe that the sole purpose of being born on this planet is to grow spiritually towards the ultimate goal of unity with God. As we live our lives, we are constantly presented with a choice between good and evil, between right and wrong. These choices become our life record and ultimately will decide what future choices are ahead of us. I believe that God gives each one of us an equal opportunity to advance spiritually. As in education, the more we make the better decisions, the more choices we will have in the future. Through God's grace and love, we don't have to pay for each of our mistakes (sins). The path of life we are on is based on both past experiences, faith and what are our needs to advance along our spiritual path to God. In the final analysis, we are involved in planning future life experiences.

I would like to relate a story from my early childhood. When I was around 12 years of age, I remember coming to my Mother and asking: "Mother, where do babies go when they die"? She answered: "Son, they are pure and innocent, and go directly to heaven". I then said: "Mother, I wish I had died as a baby, since that would guarantee me a place in heaven". Mother answered: "Son, you shouldn't think that way. By growing and maturing as a person, you will be given the opportunity to grow in God's sight". I then responded: "If that is true, why wasn't the baby given the same opportunity"? My Mother's final answer was: "Son, there are some things we don't understand now, but we will get the answer when we leave this Earth". Looking back on this, the great puzzle in life's experiences remained un-answered, unless we consider that we have existed before.

To further complicate the picture, who decided, in Biblical times, who would be born a Hebrew with the opportunity to find God, and who would be born a Philistine who would become the mortal enemies of the Hebrews, and many would be killed in combat by the "chosen people"? Another more startling example is the Passover in Moses' time. The Bible tells us that all households who put blood on their door posts would be spared from what was about to happen. That night, the angel of death struck all of the first born in Egypt, both man and beast that didn't have blood on their door entrances. The destiny of the Egyptian first-born was sealed. None would live to maturity. How was this choice made? There are countless examples of this apparent "bad luck" to this present day.

We finally come to the point in this whole discussion that as Christians, we are taught that Jesus Christ is the only doorway to God. That disqualifies and dooms the vast majority of all human beings that ever lived on this planet, to an eternal Godless future. Knowing that God is love and perfect justice, in my eyes, this cannot be. The only logical answer is that we all live many lives, and through future experiences, we will be given the opportunity to seek God through His Son, Jesus Christ.

CHAPTER 22

CREATION

This is the story of the Universe and the ant.

To understand the immensity of creation, I am going to present some very simple astronomical facts. The planet Earth and its parent Solar System is located about two thirds of the way from the center of our home galaxy known as The Milky Way. Proof that our galaxy was comprised of a very large number of stars came about through the use of a telescope the Italian scientist, Galileo, invented in the early 1600's. With this telescope, he was able to see a huge number of stars that comprise our galaxy. Several centuries later, with the development of more powerful telescopes, astronomers determined that the milky appearance in the night sky was our home galaxy. It is estimated that our galaxy contains 200 to 400 billion stars, and is about 13 billion years old. Our nearest large neighbor is the Andromeda galaxy, that contains an estimated one trillion stars, which is twice as many as our Milky Way galaxy has. Astronomers estimate that there are probably more than 170 billion galaxies in the Universe. Multiply this by the number of stars in a galaxy, and the possible planets around each star, and you end up with a number that is almost impossible to comprehend. It is like trying to understand the immensity of our Creator. To say that all of this happened accidentally is to think like a fool. Most of the world thought the earth was at the center of the Universe, and until Columbus sailed the ocean blue, most people thought our planet was flat. Poor Galileo, who was trying to prove that the earth revolved around the sun, and was persecuted by religious intolerance, and lived the rest of his life under house arrest. One final comment about the Universe. Most of all that we see through our telescopes no longer exists as we see it because light takes, in many cases, billions of years to reach us. In other words, we are looking at ancient history, and cannot imagine what is currently "out there".

This whole discussion which my wife calls too "technical", is presented to show that our little planet is like a grain of sand on the seashore of this magnificent creation. When it comes to religion, this is the so-called "gorilla in the room". This means that our religious beliefs cannot extend beyond this planet. We are left with the need to focus on our daily lives in this world, observing what we've been taught about our Creator. We shouldn't ignore, however, that we are only looking at the material one-half of creation, and that we are heading, at a great rate of speed toward the spiritual half of creation, which of course is infinite in size.

The Giant Nebula, NGC 3603

Thousands of sparkling young stars nestled within the giant nebula NGC 3603. This stellar "jewel box" is one of the most massive young star clusters in the Milky Way Galaxy. NGC 3603 is a prominent star-forming region in the Carina spiral arm of the Milky Way, about 20,000 light-years away. This image shows a young star cluster surrounded by a vast region of dust and gas. The image reveals stages in the life cycle of stars. The nebula was first discovered by Sir John Herschel in 1834. The image spans roughly 17 light-years.

Image Credit: NASA, ESA, and the Hubble Heritage

Download Image
> Full Size
> 1600 x 1200
> 1024 x 768
> 800 x 600

figure 22.1 [88]

A GLIMPSE INSIDE OUR MILKY WAY GALAXY

figure 22.2 [89]

MILKY WAY, WITH LOCATION OF OUR SUN

figure 22.3 [90]

M-101 SPIRAL GALAXY

(M-101 galaxy contains an estimated 1 trillion stars, with 100 billion like our Sun)

figure 22.4 [91]

THE ANDROMEDA GALAXY

(OUR NEAREST LARGE NEIGHBOR)

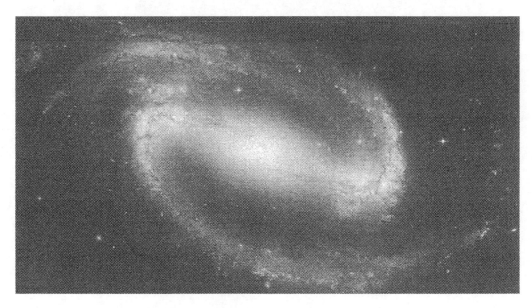

figure 22.5 [92]

BARRED SPIRAL GALAXY

(Giant, cluster galaxies, can contain 100 trillion stars)

Now that I have briefly discussed our wondrous universe, I want to tell the story of the common ant. Ants are an amazing creature. They form organized colonies where each ant has an assigned function. They send out scouts, and when a scout locates food, they leave an odor on the trail that others can follow. When the food runs out, the last ant to bring back food leaves a special odor that tells other ants that the food is all gone. After describing the glorious universe, why in the world am I writing about one of the smallest creatures on earth. The reason is that the common ant has one unusual characteristic. Although it is very intelligent, organized and capable of defending itself, it seems to be totally unaware of the giant that is looking down on them while they are busy with their daily activities. Unfortunately, this is the behavior of most of the people on this planet. They are busy-busy in their daily activities and rarely, if ever, notice the universe we live in. In living this existence, their Creator is largely ignored. We must realize that in our tiny fishbowl, there is a huge ocean outside. This expanded view will ultimately bring us closer to God.

CHAPTER 23

THE BIBLE

The Bible, without a doubt, is the greatest book ever written. A lot of things can be said about the Bible, but first and foremost, it identifies God as the only Creator. The Bible has provided, and continues to provide a road to salvation for countless numbers of people. It also inspires, consoles, guides, educates, prophesies, heals, chastises, and provides a direct path to God for all those who seek Him. I am tackling this vast subject primarily to provide the non-believer and those who are sitting on the fence with explanations that might open their minds. This is not intended as an ecclesiastical treatise on the Bible. I read the Bible in the evening, every day, before retiring for the night, and the more I read it, the more I wonder at its wisdom and inspiration. So, I'm passing along some of my own interpretations and observations that may help those seeking an answer to many of their questions I hear from time to time.

Anybody can read The Old Testament and learn about the history of the Hebrew people. This book, however, contains much more than that. It is in the very beginning of the story about the chosen people where you find some of the hardest things to understand if you believe that every written word is to be taken literally. The following are a few examples of things that puzzle me:

- Creation.

The story of the creation of our planet is too simplistic. This is the story that non-believers scoff at. Astronomers have provided ample proof that the creation of the universe was a very complex event spanning billions and billions of years. After the "Big Bang" that started the birth of our universe, this maelstrom of gasses ultimately solidified into stars, and then came the galaxies, and planets around some of the stars. This story is way above the heads of the early, uneducated inhabitants of the Earth. Keep in mind what I wrote earlier that until fairly recently, mankind believed the Earth was in the center of the universe, and that until Columbus came along, everybody believed that the Earth was flat. The story of creation goes on to say that God created vegetation before the sun was created. In my viewpoint, the most important concept in this story is that things didn't happen accidentally but rather there was a Divine Presence back of all creation.

Now we get to Adam and Eve. Genesis tells us that God liked to walk in the Garden of Eden, enjoying the cool of the day. This describes a flesh and blood God, rather than a Divine Spirit that even the whole universe could not contain. When God created Adam, He at first didn't think that man would need a woman. How in the world was mankind going to populate the Earth without a male and female? Genesis goes on to explain that the lonely Adam would need a companion, (not a co-procreator of humans). So God created Eve. The method He used to create Eve, however, was totally different from the way He created Adam, and to this day, in many parts of the world, woman is subservient to the man. The story continues telling about a serpent that had legs to walk on, had vocal cords to speak, and was highly intelligent. At this point, I want to repeat what I said earlier. It would be impossible for the Earth's early inhabitants to comprehend the story of the universe. I believe that this part of Genesis provided future early readers with a story of creation they could understand. The main concluding point is that God is the only creator and that through His Divine Wisdom that everything in the universe came into existence.

- The Nature of God.

If a person reads the Old Testament and then the New Testament, it appears as if we are getting two different descriptions of God, or even two different Gods. In the Old Testament we read that God was constantly burning with anger at the misdeeds of His chosen people. Another human attribute He had was jealousy. To top it all off, He greatly relished in massive blood sacrifices, and enjoyed the aroma of burning animals. He also would discriminate between non-blood and blood sacrifices, preferring the latter. One might ask: "Doesn't the purpose behind the sacrifice count"? To continue, we find that Old Testament personalities could argue with God. Also, He could, as we read in Exodus, harden Pharaoh's heart so that He could ultimately show Egypt His might. What happened to free will?

If we then turn to the New Testament, we find a description of God who is loving, merciful, and forgiving. How can these two opposite views define one Creator who never changes throughout eternity? The answer, I believe, is in perception. The chosen people of the Old Testament were for the most part rebellious and disobedient. The relations between God and His people followed the type of relationship that exists between a father and his disobedient child. In the New Testament, the relationship moves up much higher. We now have the Son of God among us, providing directly the example we must follow if we are to find God.

- The Nature of Temptation.

We could start with the temptation of Adam and Eve, or, more realistically, with King David and Bathsheba where David not only committed adultery but indirectly murdered Bathsheba's husband. David's temptation of wanting another man's wife was too great to resist. Because of David's belief and devotion to God, this great sin was forgiven. In the New Testament we read about how Jesus was tempted in the wilderness for forty days. What we don't pay attention to is that He was tempted a second time. We read in the Gospel according to Matthew, Chapter 26, that while He was praying in a place called Gethsemane, He asked God to spare him the crucifixion that awaited Him. His human nature at that point, knowing what lay ahead, turned him away from His mission to serve as a sacrificial lamb. He then goes on to say to God that God's will be done. After He said that, we read in the Gospel according to Luke, Chapter 22, Verse 43: "Now an angel from heaven appeared to Him, strengthening Him." From this we can see that Jesus was being tempted by the human part of His nature, to be spared the terrible physical experience just ahead of Him.

- The Nature of Sin and Evil.

All sin is disobedience of God's laws and statutes, and a turning away from Him in our daily lives. The nature and origin of evil, however, is a much more difficult subject. The Bible tells us of original sin starting with Adam and Eve. To convict all future generations of mankind because of the act of two people is hard for me to believe. When Eve took of the fruit from the tree of knowledge and gave it to Adam, the succeeding billions of people to be born were stamped with the word "sinner". Why Eve chose not to eat first from the tree of life is a mystery to me. I personally believe that just being born on this planet results in two things: (1) We are automatically given a death sentence as soon as we take our first breath; (2) we are born into a physical world that will along life's path provide us with a choice between good and evil, or to put it into contemporary language, a choice between doing the right thing and not doing the right thing. We could say that where ever we came from, our being born on this planet was equivalent to original sin. The results are the same as those sentenced on Adam and Eve. We all have to labor by the sweat of our brow, and we will all pass away.

There is no doubt that evil in all of its terrifying forms exists on this planet. Is all of this evil created and directed by a supreme evil entity called Satan or Devil? The problem that I have with this concept is that, to put it in current legal language, it makes God a co-conspirator with evil. The Bible tells us that ultimately God will tell Satan that he has created enough evil, and that He will throw him down to Earth. Poor Earth! Is that what is in its future? What about the Millennium when Christ will rule the world with peace and goodness for 1000 years? And what about Jesus's promise that the meek will inherit the Earth? And one final point. How will Satan, a spiritual being, be anchored forever more to a physical planet such as the Earth, a planet with a distinct lifetime. When we consider that we are a very small part of an immense universe, it becomes very difficult to understand this concept. The Bible is replete with the mention of Satan. It is as if Satan had to be created to explain the misdeeds of mankind. The true answer lies in our second great gift, i.e., free will. Again, a child has free will to live life as he chooses. Finally, to understand this great mystery, perhaps we should substitute the word "error", i.e., wrong choice", whenever we run across the word "Satan". After all, doesn't the Bible call him a great liar? Is it possible that his very existence is a lie?

A STATEMENT OF FAITH

I would like to state, for the record, that I was born and raised in a Christian family. At age 14, I was baptized by my Dad the old fashioned way, by submergence.

I've tried to live up to the Christian principles my Mother and Dad taught me. I believe in one Creator and in his son Jesus Christ as my personal savior. The latter part of this book was written because I have so many unanswered questions about life and where we came from. These questions and observations about the world we live in, in no way alter my basic Christian beliefs. I do believe that God has a plan for all humanity.

A 5-YEAR OLD'S BEDTIME PRAYER

Now I lay me down to sleep,
I pray the Lord my soul to keep,
May angels watch me through the night,
And keep me in their blessed sight.

Dear Lord:
Please let me have good dreams not bad.
Bless my Mom, Dad, Bebah (his brother Jeffery)
Braney (his dog),
Bless Grammy and Grandpa Al,
Bless my other family members.
Keep them healthy, happy, and safe.
Bless all my pets and pillow pets.
Bless all of my toys and my outside playground.
Thank you for our house and all other gifts you have given me.
In Jesus' name I pray. Amen.

(This is a prayer of our little 5-year old grandson, Jace Achtermann. He wrote it and prays it every night).

A POEM BY MY WIFE, LOVELLA

Sitting in a classroom with a wandering mind,

And thinking of happenings of mankind,

Where did I come from, a small boy might ask?

And where will I go because forever won't last?

And then you begin to tell him your own belief.

Look up my child, there lives a Man, his name you have heard,

He is Almighty, and can't be explained in words.

One day He was lonesome, so He said,

I'll make a world that will never be dead.

So a world He made and a fine one, I'll say,

Then He made a man from a small clump of clay.

This man was lonely,, so he made a wife,

He took one of his ribs, and gave it life.

It was then that generations began,

For colors of skin, beneath each of the same blood, ran

The red, the black, the yellow, and the white.

They were all created by the same heavenly light.

(This poem was written when Lovella was 14 years old.)

MY WONDERFUL PARENTS

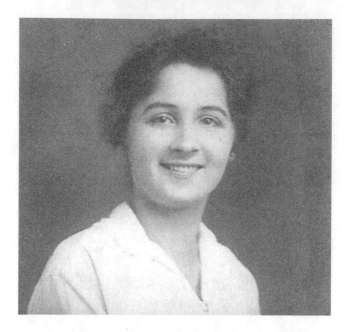

figure 23.1 [93]

MOTHER, 1917, 17 YEARS OLD

figure 23.2 [94]

DAD, 1943, 50 YEARS OLD

AL & LOVELLA BARNES
(Love, Fidelity, & Companionship)

CREDITS AND ACKNOWLEDGEMENTS

Photographs

(Endnotes)

1. figure 1.1, The Barnes Family: personal photo

2. figure 2.1, BOEING B-17 Flying Fortress, "Color Photographed B-17E in Flight". Source: U.S. Air Force

3. figure 2.2, President Franklin D. Roosevelt, "FDR in 1933". Source: U.S. Library of Congress

4. figure 2.3, "USS Indianapolis CA-35". Source: U.S. Navy

5. figure 2.4, The S.S. Argentina

6. figure 2.5, Evita Peron, "Evita color". Source: Archivo Grafico de la Nacion

7. figure 2.6, Juan Peron, "Peron Tomando un Café". Source: Soles Digital. Author: Pinelides A. Fusco

8. figure 2.7, EVITA'S CHILDREN'S VILLAGE, "Republica de los ninios3.jpg: Author: Patricio Lorente; "Wikipedia Commons", and The Creative Commons Attribution-Share Alike 2.5 Generic license

9. figure 3.1, Douglas DC 3, "Douglas DC-3, SE-CFP": Author: Towpilot; "Wikipedia Commons", under the GNU Free Documentation License, Version 1.2, and the Creative Commons Attribution-Share Alike 3.0 Unported license

10. figure 3.2, THE PAN AMERICAN FLYING CLIPPER, "Sikorsky S42 (Crop). Source: U.S. Library of Congress

11. figure 4.1, THE U. S. NAVY SB2C HELLDIVER, Curtiss SB2C Helldiver CAF.jpg: Author: Kogo; Wikipedia Commons, and the GNU Free Documentation License, Version 1.2

12. figure 4.2, Proof of American Citizenship, personal photo

13. figure 4.3, Proof that I was in the Navy, personal photo

14. figure 5.1, INTERNATIONAL SMELTING & REFINING CO., copied from a bulletin issued by the Tooele County Health Department entitled "International Smelter and Refinery Superfund Site"

15. figure 5.2, My Trusty 1934 Cheverolet, personal photo

16. figure 5.3, The Fearsome Threesome, personal photo

17. figure 5.4, MOUNT RUSHMORE, personal photo

18. figure 5.4a, OUR LITTLE BLACK DOG, personal photo

19. figure 5.5, Rube and Bob, personal photo

20. figure 5.6, COULD IT BE INDIANA JONES, personal photo

21. figure 5.7, Rube & Friend, personal photo

22. figure 5.8, MOUNT POPOCATEPETL, "Mexico-Popocatepetl.jpg": Author: Jakub Hejtmanek; "Wikipedia Commons", under the GNU Free Documentation License, Version 1.2, and the Creative Commons Attribution-Share Alike 3.0 Unported license

23. figure 5.9, DUKE CHAPEL, "Duke Chapel 4 16 05". Source: Wikipedia Commons

24. figure 7.1, The Martin P6M SeaMaster, "P6M Seamaster". Source: U.S.Navy

25. figure 7.2, THE ROCKET SCIENTIST, WERNER VON BRAUN, "Werner von Braun crop". Source: NASA

26. figure 7.3, THE SUPERSONIC BOMARC, "BOMARC". Source: U.S. Air Force

27. figure 7.4, THE CHESAPEAKE BAY BRIDGE, "Chesapeake Bay Bridge". Kent Island insert; Source: U.S. Dept. of Agriculture

28. figure 7.5, BOEING KC-135 STRATOTANKER, "100225-F-3252P-617". Source: U.S. Air Force

29. figure 7.6, BOEING B-50 SUPERFORTRESS, "B-50A Lucky Lady II in flight 1949". Source: U.S. Air Force

30. figure 7.7, BOEING B-47 STRATOJET, "B-47A". Source: U.S. Air Force

31. figure 7.8, AERO COMMANDER, "Aero Commander U-4B USAF". Source: U.S. Air Force

32. figure 7.9, REPUBLIC F-105D THUNDERCHIEF, "Republic F-105D Thunderchief USAF". Source: U.S. Air Force

33. figure 7.10, THOMAS POINT LIGHTHOUSE, Thomas Point Lighthouse Chesapeake Bay". Source: U.S. Coast Guard

34. figure 7.11, THE FIRST VIDEO TAPE RECORDER SOLD IN THE UNITED STATES, personal photo

35. figure 7.12, Working On The Video Recorder With My No.1 Technician, personal photo

36. figure 7.13, MARTIN B57A BOMBER, "Martin B-57A USAF 52-1418". Source: U.S. Air Force

37. figure 8.1, THE APOLLO COMMAND/SERVICE MODULE, "Apollo CSM lunar Orbit". Source: NASA

38. figure 8.2, THE APOLLO LUNAR MODULE, "Apollo 16 LM". Source: NASA

39. figure 8.3, SATURN V – APOLLO MOON ROCKET, "KSC-69pc-442". Source: NASA

40. figure 8.4, APOLLO 11 FLIGHT CREW (1ˢᵗ LUNAR LANDING), "Apollo 11". Source: NASA

41. figure 8.5, DEKE SLAYTON, APOLLO CHIEF ASTRONAUT, personal photo

42. figure 8.6, ASTRONAUTS ED WHITE, GUS GRISSOM, ROGER CHAFFEE, "A1 Prayer". Source: NASA

43. figure 8.7, ASTRONAUT EDWARD GIVENS, "Edward Galen Givens". Source: NASA

44. figure 9.1, Million Dollar Award, personal photo

45. figure 12.1, BRASILIA, THE NEW CAPITAL OF BRAZIL, "Montagem Brasilia.jpg": Author: Heitor Carvalho Jorge; "Wikipedia Commons", under the GNU Free Documentation License, Version 1.2, and the Creative Commons Attribution-Share Alike 3.0 Unported license

46. figure 13.1, CHIEF JUSTICE EARL WARREN, "Earl Warren". Source: Harvard Law School Library

47. figure 13.2, ANDREI GROMYKO, "Andrej Gromyko 1967". Source: Wikipedia Commons

48. figure 13.3, ARGENTINE PRESIDENT FRONDIZI & FAMILY, "Arturo Frondizi". Source: Archivo Grafico de la Nacion

49. figure 13.4, DON BARNES WITH PRESIDENT EISENHOWER, personal photo

50. figure 13.5, JACK KENNEDY VISITING IN COSTA RICA, personal photo

51. figure 13.6, PRESIDENT JACK KENNEDY, "John F. Kennedy White House Color Photo Portrait". Source: U.S. Gov't

52. figure 13.7, JACKIE KENNEDY, "JBK in Fort Worth (11-22-63)". Source: U.S. Gov't

53. figure 13.8, MEXICAN PRESIDENT LOPEZ MATEOS

54. figure 13.9, BAY OF PIGS, "Bay of Pigs". User: Zleitzen; "Wikipedia Commons", under the GNU Free Documentation License, Version 1.2, and the Creative Commons Attribution-Share Alike 3.0 Unported license

55. figure 13.10, BAY OF PIGS 2, "Bay of Pigs". User: Zleitzen; "Wikipedia Commons", under the GNU Free Documentation License, Version 1.2, and the Creative Commons Attribution-Share Alike 3.0 Unported license

56. figure 13.11, JACK & JACKIE KENNEDY @ THE ORANGE BOWL, personal photo

57. figure 13.12, ARTICLE IN THE SAN JUAN STAR, "J.F.K's Interpreter Stunned". Source: The San Juan Star, Tuesday, November 26, 1963

58. figure 13.13, Don Barnes is in the middle, just back of the Kennedy's, obtained from an AP Wirephoto, Syracuse Herald-Journal, 7-2-62

59. figure 13.14, PRESIDENT JOHNSON WITH THE PRESIDENT OF URUGUAY, personal photo

60. figure 13.15, PRESIDENT NIXON (left) WITH LUIS ECHEVERRIA, Richard Nixon, Luis Echeverria 1972-06-15". Source: National Archives

61. figure 13.16, RICHARD M. NIXON, "Richard Nixon". Source: U.S. Gov't

62. figure 13.17, GERALD FORD, "Gerald Ford". Source: U.S. Gov't

63. figure 13.18, PRESIDENT NIXON AND PRESIDENT ECHEVERRIA, personal photo

64. figure 13.19, JIMMY CARTER, "Jimmy Carter Portrait 2". Source: U.S. Gov't

88. figure 22.1, A GLIMPSE INSIDE OUR MILKY WAY GALAXY, "The Giant Nebula, NGC 3603": Source: NASA, ESA and the Hubble Heritage

89. figure 22.2, MILKY WAY, WITH LOCATION OF OUR SUN, "Galactic longitude": Source: NASA

90. figure 22.3, M-101 SPIRAL GALAXY, "Hubble2005-01-barred-spiral-galaxy-NGC1300": Source: NASA and ESA

91. figure 22.4, THE ANDROMEDA GALAXY, "Andromeda Galaxy (with h-alpha).jpg: Author: Adam Evan; Creative Commons Attribution 2.0 Generic license; "Wikipedia Commons",

92. figure 22.5, BARRED SPIRAL GALAXY, "Hubble2005-01-barred-spiral-galaxy-NGC1300": Source: NASA and ESA; "Wikipedia Commons",

93. figure 23.1, MOTHER, personal photo

94. figure 23.2, DAD, personal photo

The following figures numbers were obtained from "Wikipedia, The Free Encyclopedia". These photos were listed as being in the "Public Domain"
2.1, 2.2, 2.3, 2.5, 2.6, 3.2, 5.9, 7.1, 7.2, 7.3, 7.4, 7.5, 7.6, 7.7, 7.8, 7.9, 7.10, 7.13, 8.1, 8.2, 8.3, 8.4, 8.5, 8.6, 8.7, 13.1, 13.3, 13.6, 13.7, 13.8, 13.9, .10, 13.15, 13.16, 13.17, 13.19, 13.20, 13.22, 13.24, 13.25, 13026, 13.28, 15.1, 15.2, 15.3, 15.4, 15.5, 15.6, 15.7, 17.1, 22.1, 22.2, 22.3

Text

Text between figure 2.2 and 2.3: "The Sinking of the USS Indianapolis, 1945". Source: Eyewitness to History.